W9-ANP-816

The Formative Assessment Action Plan

Nancy **Frey**
Douglas **Fisher**

The **Formative** **Assessment** Action Plan

Practical
Steps to More
Successful
Teaching
and Learning

Alexandria, Virginia USA

1703 N. Beauregard St. • Alexandria, VA 22311-1714 USA
Phone: 800-933-2723 or 703-578-9600 • Fax: 703-575-5400
Web site: www.ascd.org • E-mail: member@ascd.org
Author guidelines: www.ascd.org/write

Gene R. Carter, *Executive Director*; Judy Zimny, *Chief Program Development Officer*; Nancy Modrak, *Publisher*; Scott Willis, *Director, Book Acquisitions & Development*; Julie Houtz, *Director, Book Editing & Production*; Jamie Greene, *Editor*; Georgia Park, *Graphic Designer*; Mike Kalyan, *Production Manager*; Sarah Plumb, *Production Specialist*; BMWW, *Typesetter*.

© 2011 by ASCD. All rights reserved. No part of this publication may be reproduced or transmitted in any form or by any means, electronic or mechanical, including photocopy, recording, or any information storage and retrieval system, without permission from ASCD. Readers who wish to duplicate material copyrighted by ASCD may do so for a small fee by contacting the Copyright Clearance Center (CCC), 222 Rosewood Dr., Danvers, MA 01923, USA (phone: 978-750-8400; fax: 978-646-8600; Web: www.copyright.com). For requests to reprint rather than photocopy, contact ASCD's permissions office: 703-575-5749 or permissions@ascd.org. Translation inquiries: translations@ascd.org.

Printed in the United States of America. Cover art © 2011 by ASCD. ASCD publications present a variety of viewpoints. The views expressed or implied in this book should not be interpreted as official positions of the Association.

All Web links in this book are correct as of the publication date below but may have become inactive or otherwise modified since that time. If you notice a deactivated or changed link, please e-mail books@ascd.org with the words "Link Update" in the subject line. In your message, please specify the Web link, the book title, and the page number on which the link appears.

PAPERBACK ISBN: 978-1-4166-1169-1   ASCD product #111013   n5/11
Also available as an e-book (see Books in Print for the ISBNs).

Quantity discounts for the paperback edition only: 10–49 copies, 10%; 50+ copies, 15%; for 1,000 or more copies, call 800-933-2723, ext. 5634, or 703-575-5634. For desk copies: member@ascd.org.

Library of Congress Cataloging-in-Publication Data

Frey, Nancy, 1959–
   The formative assessment action plan : practical steps to more successful teaching and learning / Nancy Frey and Douglas Fisher.
      p. cm.
   Includes bibliographical references and index.
   ISBN 978-1-4166-1169-1 (pbk. : alk. paper)
   1. Educational tests and measurements.   2. Teacher–student relationships.   3. Communication in education.   4. Effective teaching.   I. Fisher, Douglas, 1965–   II. Title.
   LB3051.F735 2011
   371.102—dc22
                                                                    2011000968

20 19 18   4 5 6 7 8 9 10 11 12

THE FORMATIVE ASSESSMENT ACTION PLAN

Practical Steps to More Successful Teaching and Learning

1

Creating a Formative Assessment System

"I don't know how you're going to learn this, but it's on the test," said the professor of a graduate class on neuroanatomy that Doug was taking.

The teacher's words clearly articulated one perspective about education: Students should study and learn the content assigned to them. Her statement suggested that the teacher's job is to provide information and the students' job is to learn it, whatever way they can. When his teacher implied that the responsibility for learning rested solely on the students, Doug's confidence plummeted. Having looked at intricate pictures of the human brain, Doug was already questioning how he was going to learn this information. Now his teacher was telling him that she, too, didn't know how he (or any other student in the class) would learn it.

Understand that Doug was highly motivated to learn this content, and understand that his teacher was armed with the latest technology and instructional methods. The teacher was caring and passionate about her subject area, and, further, she had clearly communicated her high expectations at the outset of the course and summarized information weekly. Were these measures enough to ensure that Doug, and the other members of the class, reached high levels of understanding? Simply put, no. Even though high-quality instruction, innovative technology, motivation, high expectations, and passion are important in the teaching and learning process, they are not sufficient to ensure that learning occurs.

What was missing from this scenario—and from the entire class experience—was a formative assessment system. The teacher needed to establish learning goals, check for understanding, provide feedback, and then align future instruction with the students' performance. She needed an instructional framework that allowed her to feed-forward, not just provide feedback.

A Formative Assessment System

Feedback, when used as part of a formative assessment system, is a powerful way to improve student achievement. Feedback by itself, though, is less useful. As John Hattie and Helen Timperley note, "Feedback has no effect in a vacuum; to be powerful in its effect, there must be a learning context to which feedback is addressed" (2007, p. 82).

Hattie and Timperley propose a formative assessment system that has three components: feed-up, feedback, and feed-forward (see Figure 1.1). Feed-up ensures that students understand the purpose of the assignment, task, or lesson, including how they will be assessed. Feedback provides students with information about their successes and needs. Feed-forward guides student learning based on performance data. All three are required if students are to learn at high levels. Each of these three components has a guiding question for teachers and students:

- Where am I going? (feed-up)
- How am I doing? (feedback)
- Where am I going next? (feed-forward)

Imagine Doug's teacher establishing the purpose for one of her classes, perhaps something like this: *To use cytoarchitecture to identify locations in the cerebral cortex.* She might then check for understanding, maybe through an audience response system, and provide individuals and the class with feedback. For example, she might ask, "Do the various regions of the brain contain the same number of cellular levels?" This dichotomous question has an answer

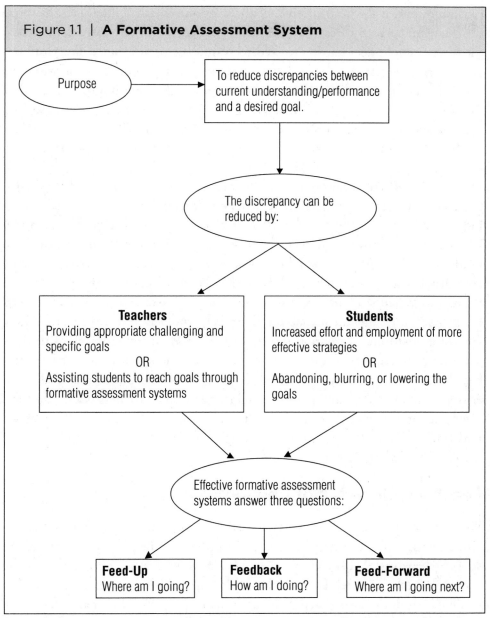

Figure 1.1 | **A Formative Assessment System**

Purpose → To reduce discrepancies between current understanding/performance and a desired goal.

The discrepancy can be reduced by:

Teachers
Providing appropriate challenging and specific goals
OR
Assisting students to reach goals through formative assessment systems

Students
Increased effort and employment of more effective strategies
OR
Abandoning, blurring, or lowering the goals

Effective formative assessment systems answer three questions:

Feed-Up
Where am I going?

Feedback
How am I doing?

Feed-Forward
Where am I going next?

Source: From *Visible learning: A synthesis of over 800 meta-analyses relating to achievement* (p. 176), by J. Hattie, 2009, New York: Routledge. Copyright 2009 by Routledge. Adapted with permission.

(*yes*), and students would receive feedback about whether they had answered the question correctly. Based on the number of correct and incorrect responses, the teacher could decide what to feed-forward. The performance data from the class might suggest that the teacher needs to provide additional information and instruction to the whole class. Alternatively, the data might suggest that the teacher needs to ask specific students to elaborate on their answers so that she can determine the source of their misunderstanding. Then again, the data might suggest that the class has a good grasp on this content and is ready to move on.

When all three components of a formative assessment system are present, there is a give-and-take between teachers and students that facilitates learning. The absence of any one component places learning at risk. For example, when students do not understand the purpose of a lesson (feed-up), they are unlikely to demonstrate their best effort. Without a clear purpose, students are not motivated and do not see the relevance of the content they're expected to master. When students are not assessed or do not receive assessment results (feedback), they are unsure about their performance and assume that they are doing just fine. They are unlikely to make mid-course corrections in their learning processes and understanding. When teachers fail to plan instruction based on student performance (feed-forward), misconceptions are reinforced, errors go unaddressed, and gaps in knowledge persist. Teachers march through their pacing guides and continue to "teach" while students passively observe. Unfortunately, when this is the case, teachers remain oblivious to the lack of real learning their students are doing.

Feedback Alone Is Not Enough

We have argued that formative assessment is a system with three inter-related components and that no one component alone is sufficient to ensure student learning. We want to take that one step further and focus on the ways in which feedback by itself is problematic. We have already noted that feedback should not be used in a vacuum. In part, this is because feedback is external to the learner; it is "external regulation," meaning that a student is responding because of something happening to him or her from the outside, rather than responding intrinsically or internally (Ryan & Deci, 2000). Although students may occasionally use external feedback in their internal regulations, it takes more than feedback to ensure that internal regulation occurs.

External regulation is not the only reason that isolated feedback is ineffective. Another reason is that it transfers responsibility for further learning and performance improvement back to the learner. Consider the ubiquitous research paper. Students typically work on these projects for an extended length of time, maybe even getting peer editing and feedback. Finally, the due date arrives, and the teacher takes the stack of papers home to grade. Some days later, the papers are returned with feedback. What do students do with this feedback? Anyone who's been in school knows that students either recycle the paper or, if required, make the noted changes and resubmit the paper for another round of review. The teacher has likely spent a great deal of time writing comments, but this time seems wasted when students throw away their work or simply correct the mistakes the teacher identified for them. They haven't really learned from their mistakes.

The problem bears repeating. *Feedback reassigns responsibility back to the learner.* Think of a recent project on which you have received feedback. After you received the feedback, did you realize that it was, once again, up to you to figure out the next steps? Were you frustrated with this experience? Did you say to yourself, "Now I have to create another one, only to be judged again? Why can't she just tell me what she wants?" If this has happened to you, you've experienced the abrupt shift of responsibility that we're talking about.

This is not to say that we don't want students to assume increasing responsibility; we do. It's just that increasing responsibility should be planned, based on student confidence and competence. We don't want students to suddenly be responsible for the first time when they make mistakes. Rather, a sophisticated formative assessment system built on a solid instructional framework should be in place from the beginning.

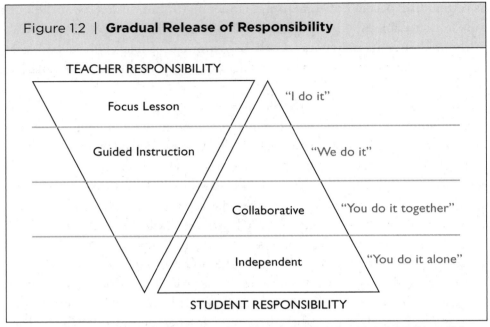

Figure 1.2 | **Gradual Release of Responsibility**

TEACHER RESPONSIBILITY

Focus Lesson — "I do it"

Guided Instruction — "We do it"

Collaborative — "You do it together"

Independent — "You do it alone"

STUDENT RESPONSIBILITY

Source: From *Better learning through structured teaching: A framework for the gradual release of responsibility* (p. 4), by D. Fisher and N. Frey, 2008, Alexandria, VA: ASCD. Copyright 2008 by ASCD. Reprinted with permission.

The Gradual Release of Responsibility Framework

A formative assessment system is only as good as the instructional framework on which it rests. No formative assessment system can compensate for poor instruction. Neither does simply having an instructional framework ensure that students will learn; both a framework and a system are required. The instructional framework we recommend is based on a gradual release of responsibility from teachers to students (Fisher & Frey, 2008a; Pearson & Gallagher, 1983) and includes five distinct components (see Figure 1.2).

Establishing Purpose

Every lesson must have an established purpose. This purpose can be in the form of a goal or objective, provided that the students know what that goal or objective is. The established purpose can have different components, such as content versus language (which will be more fully addressed in Chapter 2). Establishing purpose is important for many reasons, including alerting students to important information and keeping the teacher from getting off topic by discussing tangential information. In a formative assessment system, the purpose drives both feedback and feed-forward. Most people agree that it's not fair to assess or test students on things that haven't been taught. Sometimes students don't get the purpose of the lesson, and, in those cases, it's not fair to assess students on things that haven't been clearly established as important.

Consider these two examples. In one classroom, the teacher has students working on projects, but they don't know why or what is expected of them. There is no learning goal or purpose. In this class, the feedback students receive may be meaningless. In another classroom, the teacher has students working on projects with a clearly communicated purpose: to understand how sonar is used to determine water depths. When the teacher checks for understanding, the feedback is aligned with this purpose and the teacher can provide additional instruction to students who make errors, feeding forward until they understand the content.

Teacher Modeling

School is more than a pile of discrete facts that students have to memorize; it's about thinking, questioning, and reflecting. As apprentices, students need examples of the kinds of thinking that experts do in order to begin to approximate those habits of mind. Thinking is a complex cognitive process that is largely invisible. To make it visible, teachers model through a think-aloud in which they "open up their minds" and let students see how they go about solving the various problems of school, from quadratic equations to decoding a word. As Gerald Duffy points out, "The only way to model thinking is to talk about how to do it. That is, we provide a verbal description of the thinking one does or, more accurately, an *approximation* of the thinking involved" (2003, p. 11).

In a formative assessment system, teacher modeling serves to highlight the processes that students should use to complete tasks and assignments. It's less about the specific content and more about the ways in which experts in different disciplines go about their work. As we will explore in greater detail, formative assessment systems require attention to more than the correct response. Feedback and feed-forward also focus on the processes that students use as learners and thinkers, as well as their self-regulation and self-monitoring. Teacher modeling, through think-alouds, can provide students with examples of "self-generated thoughts, feelings, and actions that are planned and cyclically adapted to the attainment of personal goals" (Zimmerman, 2000, p. 14) such that students are responding to the feedback and future instruction they receive about learning.

Guided Instruction

In each lesson, the teacher must guide students toward increased understanding. This happens through the systematic use of questions, prompts, and cues. In this phase, questions are used to check for understanding. When a student's response indicates a misconception or an error, the teacher prompts the student. Prompts are cognitive or metacognitive and focus on getting the learner to think. If prompts fail to resolve the misconception or error, the teacher provides a cue. Cues shift the learner's attention to a resource that may help. As we will see in greater detail in Chapter 5, guided instruction is difficult to do in a whole-class format and works better in addressing the needs individual students present as they learn.

In a formative assessment system, guided instruction is an opportune time to provide students with feedback while also providing additional instruction. In this way, guided instruction plays a pivotal role in a formative assessment system as teachers feed-forward instruction based on real-time student responses. Consider the following exchange between a teacher and a small group of students having difficulty with the concept of writing mathematical sentences as inequalities.

> **Teacher**: Tell me more about your answer. Read to me what you've written.
> **Alexis**: The sentence says "Twenty minus the product of four and a number x is less than four." [$20 - 4x < 4$]
> **Teacher**: Yes, it does. So what did your group write on the chart paper?

Brandon: Right here. [points]

Teacher: Can you read that to me? Not from the projector but from your chart paper?

Justin: We wrote twenty minus four plus x is less than four. [20 – 4 + x < 4]

Teacher: Did that sound the same as when Alexis read it?

All: Yeah?

Teacher: Think about the word *product*.

Alexis: That's to multiply.

Justin: But we didn't multiply.

Brandon: Where do we multiply?

Alexis: Maybe right here? [points to the minus sign]

Teacher: Be careful. You might want to read it again.

Alexis: Twenty minus the product of four and a number x is less than four. Oh, wait, first we have to write 20 and then minus.

Justin: Then it says *product*, so we have to multiply. But you can't have multiply next to minus.

Teacher: [Cups her hands around the words "the product of four and a number x."]

Brandon: Wait. Look. It's 4x, not minus four plus x.

Alexis: Oh, it's 20 – 4x < 4. That's right, huh?

Justin: It is, now read it again. It's just like the sentence up there. [points to projected problem set]

This brief exchange allows the teacher to prompt and cue such that students experience success and complete the task. Will they need additional instruction? Probably. That's what formative assessment systems are all about: reducing discrepancies between current understandings and a desired goal (Hattie, 2009). Feedback alone would probably not have resulted in new understanding.

Productive Group Work

Though students stand to learn a lot from and with their teachers, they are unlikely to consolidate that understanding unless they also work alongside peers in creating and producing something. Importantly, creating is now considered the highest-order thinking task in the Bloom's taxonomy revised for the 21st century (see Figure 1.3). Creating something requires that students use their

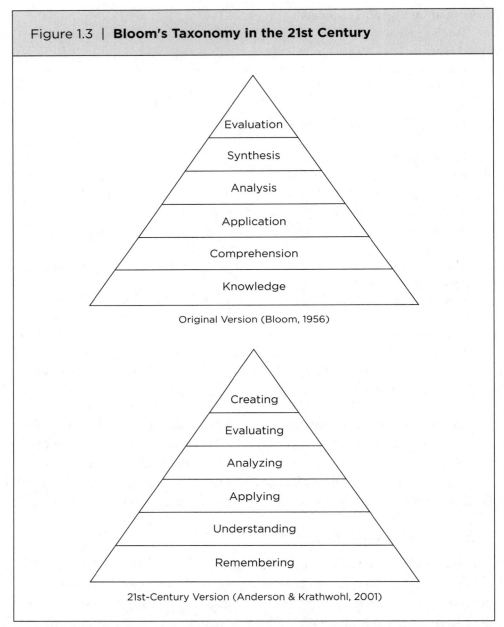

Figure 1.3 | Bloom's Taxonomy in the 21st Century

Original Version (Bloom, 1956)

- Evaluation
- Synthesis
- Analysis
- Application
- Comprehension
- Knowledge

21st-Century Version (Anderson & Krathwohl, 2001)

- Creating
- Evaluating
- Analyzing
- Applying
- Understanding
- Remembering

Source: From *Guided instruction. How to develop confident and successful learners* (p. 11), by D. Fisher and N. Frey, 2010, Alexandria, VA: ASCD. Copyright 2010 by ASCD. Reprinted with permission.

prior knowledge in new ways and that they rally resources to complete the task. As Matthew Crawford argues in *Shop Class as Soulcraft* (2009), thinking should not be separated from doing. It is the doing that solidifies understanding. Of course, educators have known this for a long time, but group work got a bad reputation because we have all experienced bad examples of this good idea. How many times have we been assigned to a group, just to do all of the work and watch others share the credit for it? That's not the productive group work we're talking about, nor is it the cooperative learning that David Johnson and Roger Johnson (1999) envisioned. The key to productive group work is individual accountability. Each member of the group must produce something based on the group's interaction. It is when students work alongside their peers that they interact, using academic language and argumentation skills.

Figure 1.4 contains an example of a product from a productive group work task in a government class. The example is one of the products from the group; each student produced his or her own notes. In this case, students were reading a text about the importance of writing letters to elected officials. Each student

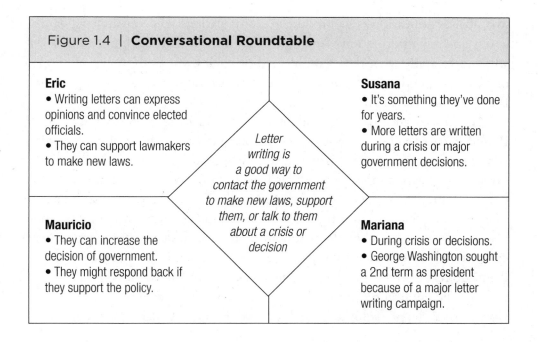

Figure 1.4 | **Conversational Roundtable**

Eric
• Writing letters can express opinions and convince elected officials.
• They can support lawmakers to make new laws.

Susana
• It's something they've done for years.
• More letters are written during a crisis or major government decisions.

Letter writing is a good way to contact the government to make new laws, support them, or talk to them about a crisis or decision

Mauricio
• They can increase the decision of government.
• They might respond back if they support the policy.

Mariana
• During crisis or decisions.
• George Washington sought a 2nd term as president because of a major letter writing campaign.

took notes about the reading in the upper left quadrant of the conversation roundtable. Then, as each member of the group discussed the reading, the other members took notes in a corresponding quadrant. When the group completed its reading and discussion, each person wrote a single-sentence summary in the middle of the paper.

In a formative assessment system, the work students create during a productive group session serves as excellent fodder for checking understanding. The instructor reviews these work products against the lesson's purpose to determine which students need additional instruction (as will be described in the subsequent chapters of this book). For example, even a quick review of Eric's conversation roundtable suggests that he understands this content and that the group had a very interesting conversation while creating notes. Following this review, the teacher modeled his own search for his elected officials, examined the officials' perspectives on specific issues, and then chose a topic on which to write a letter to an elected official.

Independent Tasks

The goal of education is to produce lifelong learners who can independently access and use information. Thus, each lesson must include opportunities for students to apply what they have learned on their own. Both in-class and out-of-class independent tasks provide students with opportunities to apply what they have learned.

The key to effective independent work lies in timing. Independent work should be used when students have demonstrated some level of success with content in the presence of their teacher and peers. Here's what doesn't work: homework assigned just after students have been introduced to content. If, for example, students were just introduced to methods for calculating the slope of a line or adding fractions, it is probably best not to assign homework on that content on the same day—because that homework is premature in this instructional cycle. It's not that homework is bad or evil; it's just that it must come when students are ready. In a formative assessment system, independent work allows for practice and application. It can also serve as a review for determining if students have grasped the prerequisite content or if additional instruction is necessary.

The components of a gradual release of responsibility model do not have to occur in a specific order to be effective. Take, for example, a lesson in which the teacher starts with students independently writing a journal entry in response to the question "How are we connected to our environment?" When the timer rings, the teacher has students work in triads to create a visual representation of their collective ideas. As part of this productive group work, each member of the group writes in a different color so the teacher can track each student's contributions. As the groups work, the teacher meets with small groups for guided instruction, asking questions and then prompting and cueing their responses. After meeting with several groups, the teacher identifies an area of need and gains students' attention. In this think-aloud, the teacher models his or her understanding of the word *connected* and the various ways that things can be connected, both physically and metaphorically. The teacher then establishes the purpose of the lesson and invites students to return to their groups and complete their charts, taking into account the additional information provided.

Again, the order of components is not important. What is important is that the teacher has an instructional framework that allows him or her to identify instructional needs, provide students with feedback, and plan appropriate instruction.

Looking Back, Looking Forward

We've introduced a system for formative assessment that provides teachers with a way to take action on student performance data. This system includes feed-up, feedback, and feed-forward, such that students understand a lesson's purpose and goal, are given information about their successes and needs, and experience high-quality instruction that closes the gap between what they know and can do and what is expected of them.

We do know that there is more information collected about students than ever before *and* that most of it is not used to make instructional decisions— probably because teachers spend too much time on student feedback and not enough time on feed-up and feed-forward. As we have noted, an exclusive focus on feedback is ineffective because it transfers the responsibility back to students exactly when they are struggling. Instead, we need an instructional framework that allows us to use performance data to make future instructional decisions. Our instructional framework, based on the gradual release of responsibility, provides an intentional way for teachers to increase student responsibility at appropriate times and reassume responsibility as needed.

In the next chapter, we turn our attention to the first part of the system—feed-up. We will explore the ways in which a lesson's purpose can be established and why a clearly communicated purpose is important. We will also investigate the role that motivation plays in student learning as well as how goal-setting can ensure that students become intrinsically motivated and exhibit internal regulation of their learning.

Feed-Up: Where Am I Going?

Not too long ago, Doug set a goal for himself—run a marathon to benefit leukemia research. Part of his motivation was altruistic, because he feels strongly about the importance of this cause. Part of it was social, because a number of his high school students and fellow teachers expressed interest in participating in the event as volunteers or walkers. Doug's competitive nature also played a role: he wanted to be the top fund-raiser for the run. Also, we can't overlook the importance of the sense of personal accomplishment to be gained from completing such a daunting task.

Several factors came into play during the period leading up to the event. For one, he had to find various ways to motivate himself. "I'm going to run a marathon in June," he told anyone who would listen. Doug realized that this provided some public accountability and helped with his fund-raising efforts. "Less than 1 percent of the population ever completes a marathon," he told others, furthering his goal to be a part of this elite group. With assistance from the sponsoring organization, he established a training plan and documented his progress. The training plan was systematic and incremental, and most important, it mapped out a path to his goal. Doug also talked with other long-distance runners to gain insights about equipment, training, and nutrition.

We see parallels between Doug's approach to running a marathon and the dynamics of teaching and learning in the classroom. Presentation of information is important—in fact, we will devote an entire chapter of this book to the importance of a gradual release of responsibility model of instruction. Here's what's key: Interleaved between instruction and attainment are the intrinsic and extrinsic factors that motivate students and propel them forward. In this chapter, we will explain a vital aspect of the teaching and learning cycle: feeding up to establish purpose, increase motivation, and set goals.

Feed-Up in the Instructional Cycle

Feed-up lies at the heart of teaching since it makes the student a partner in the business of learning and creating. It also addresses some of the individual variables that make each learner unique, especially when it comes to motivation. As any experienced teacher will tell you, what motivates one student may not work for another. The feed-up process addresses the "Where am I going?" question that students and teachers ask.

Think about a trip you've been on, perhaps to visit relatives in another state. Once you knew where you were going, you could decide how best to get there, how much time it would take, and what you would need along the way. You likely made mid-course corrections as the trip unfolded—after all, who hasn't been inconvenienced by transportation providers or traffic? When you saw your relatives' smiling faces, you clearly understood that you had made it to where you wanted to go. Like any journey, part of the learning process is to decide where you want to go. That's what this chapter is about.

The answer to the "Where am I going?" question should be jointly shared by teacher and student. In a traditional classroom, the teacher assumes the responsibility for identifying *what* will be learned and *when*, thereby leaving students to play a passive role in their learning. A student who asks, "Will this be on the test?" is desperately seeking to take back some of this responsibility, albeit in a limited way. Jay McTighe and Ken O'Connor describe three elements that shape learners' perceptions of their ability to learn:

1. *Task clarity*—when they clearly understand the learning goal and know how teachers will evaluate their learning.

2. *Relevance*—when they think the learning goals and assessments are meaningful and worth learning.

3. *Potential for success*—when they believe that they can successfully learn and meet the evaluative expectations. (2005, p. 15)

That's why attention to each of these factors—establishing purpose, increasing motivation, and setting goals—is critical to the process of learning. When each factor is carefully attended to, students take a more active role in their learning.

Establishing Purpose

Motivating students to become actively involved in their learning begins with establishing a purpose. In too many schools, the only apparent purpose is compliance—in other words, "You're going to learn this because *I* said so." Although obedience may hook some students (at least for a while), it is likely to miss many others. Those missed students are often the high-profile ones who exhibit social and behavioral problems and regularly get themselves into trouble.

A lesson's purpose lays out the content of what will be learned, the learner's role in what will be accomplished, and the expectations for the interactions. We call these the content purpose, language purpose, and social purpose (Fisher, Frey, & Rothenberg, 2008). Taken together, these elements explain what will be learned today, what the students will do with the content, and how they will work with others to accomplish these tasks. It should be noted that *today* is the operative word here. We've seen content, language, and social purposes that are too broad and therefore not perceived as doable by the learner. Consider the two versions seen in Figure 2.1.

The non-examples are not much good for describing what the learner will learn *today*. Although they may be useful as representing larger skills or concepts, they are likely to leave the learner feeling as though they are not attainable. Also, the non-examples lack the level of specificity that engenders

Figure 2.1	**Example and Non-Example of Purpose Statements**	
Purpose Statements	**Example**	**Non-Example**
Content	Learn the properties of halogens.	Learn how to use the periodic table.
Language	Compare and contrast the halogen elements using a graphic organizer, and discuss these similarities and differences with your lab partner.	Use logic and evidence to formulate explanations.
Social	Work collaboratively with your partner to submit a revised version of the graphic organizer.	Be nice.

confidence in students' perceptions about whether they are making forward progress. Just as it would be foolish to tell Doug to run a marathon and then leave him on his own to figure out how, there is limited effectiveness to simply stating ambitious objectives that don't include a plan for what to do today.

On the other hand, the examples provide the learner with a plan of action concerning what will be learned, what the learner will do with the content, and the ways he or she will interact with others in the process of learning it. A student entering a chemistry class might hear this:

> Today we're going to learn about halogens, a family of elements on the periodic table. We're going to examine their unique characteristics, and you're going to discuss with your lab partner the ways that halogens are similar to and different from other elements on the chart. The two of you will develop a graphic organizer of your choice that shows how these halogens compare with other families of elements.

Consider the intended audience for the statement above—students—and then consider learning objectives. Though it is true that most lessons are organized according to objectives, objectives are primarily constructed with the teacher in mind, for they serve as an effective way to plan a lesson. However, lesson objectives "stay on the page"; objectives must be translated into purpose statements, like the one above, that are then expressed to the learners themselves. In some classrooms, especially those with young students, these purpose statements might also be posted on the board for reference. For example, in a kindergarten classroom, the teacher might have a content purpose related to the way that stories are constructed. The focus for the day might be:

> After hearing a story, identify the characters, settings, and important events.

One of the ways that purpose statements can be communicated to students is through the use of "I can" statements (Au, Carroll, & Scheu, 1995). These are statements of future achievement that communicate expected learning outcomes in student-friendly language. They do not reflect what the student can currently do but, rather, what they will be able to do after following instruction. As Kathryn Au notes, teachers plan instruction with an objective or purpose in mind, but these expectations "may require rewording before they can be readily understood by students, particularly those in the lower grades" (2010, p. 18). An "I can" statement for the kindergarten purpose above might be "I can retell a story and name the characters, setting, and important events." In some cases, like this example, "I can" statements are closely connected with purpose statements. In other cases, the purpose is more abstract and students are not always sure what they are expected to learn. A sample list of "I can" statements can be found in Figure 2.2.

Establishing purpose facilitates the process of moving from initial learning to transfer of learning. In the chemistry example above, the content purpose *(unique characteristics of halogens)* represents initial learning. More permanent learning is measured by the ability to apply what is learned. This application of learning is called transfer, and the statement alerts students to the ways they will accomplish this today through the language purpose *(discuss the ways that halogens are similar to and different from other elements and develop a graphic organizer that shows how these halogens compare with other families of elements).* Of course, transfer of learning doesn't automatically occur just because you announced it. In the book *How People Learn*, the authors caution that "[i]t is

Figure 2.2 | Sample "I Can" Statements

Reading

I can retell a story in my own words.

I can make meaning when I read a variety of texts.

I can make connections between my own life and what I am reading.

I can make connections within and between texts.

I can figure out a theme from my reading.

Writing

I can write to communicate my ideas.

I can use writing for different purposes and audiences.

I can show "me" in my writing.

Discussion

I can contribute to a good book club discussion.

    (a) I can stay on topic when I talk.

    (b) I can share my feelings and ideas.

    (c) I can respect others' ideas and opinions.

    (d) I can build on others' ideas.

    (e) I can bring others into the discussion.

Evaluation

I can show and/or tell what I learned and how I learned it.

Culture

I can use artifacts to describe

    (a) my own cultural heritage,

    (b) others' cultures, and

    (c) similarities and differences across cultures.

I can define culture and how cultures change.

Source: From "Thinking for ourselves: Literacy learning in a diverse teacher inquiry network," by T. E. Raphael, S. Florio-Ruane, and M. J. Kehus, 2001, *The Reading Teacher, 54*(6), pp. 596–607. Copyright 2001 by the International Reading Association, www.reading.org. Reprinted with permission.

important to view transfer as a dynamic process that requires learners to actively choose and evaluate strategies, consider resources, and receive feedback" (Bransford, Brown, & Cocking, 2000, p. 66). The purpose statement sets up a schema for what will be learned and how it will be applied.

It is that construction of a schema that is essential for all learners but is especially important for English language learners (ELLs). At various times, and especially when academic language is used, ELLs may need to rely on internal translations between their first and second languages to make sense of instruction. In addition, the ability of an ELL to process and understand speech does not occur uniformly across types of words. In fact, intermediate ELLs often process content words more accurately than function words (such as conjunctions, prepositions, and articles). An ELL in that chemistry classroom is more likely to accurately interpret *halogen*, *discuss*, and *graphic organizer* than he or she is to understand *with*, *to*, and *on* (Dutro & Moran, 2003). A purpose statement fosters further understanding of these function words by pairing them with the actions and gestures used by the teacher, providing learners with "multiple examples of natural language in use" (Field, 2008, p. 429).

Establishing purpose is one element in a feed-up system that views the learner as an active partner. Another element is motivation, both internal and external. Motivation is linked with purpose as students decide if they are interested in the purpose that has been established. That's not to say that students only study things that are interesting to them individually. They also have to learn specific things in specific grades. We have standards for different grade levels and content disciplines. It's up to the teacher to ensure that the purpose for achieving those standards is relevant and that students are invited into the content.

Increasing Motivation

Motivation and its effect on learning has long been the subject of educational research. Motivation is considered vital because it "affects the amount of time that people are willing to devote to learning" (Bransford et al., 2000, p. 60).

A number of conditions can increase or decrease one's level of motivation. The first is the perceived relevance of the information. Think of the safety instructions given before each airplane flight. The flight attendant presents important information to the passengers, and this information is mostly ignored—yet this same information would be critical if an emergency erupted. Passengers would be riveted to the flight attendant's instructions and would faithfully execute every command. The difference is perceived relevance. A smoke-filled airplane cabin motivates passengers to learn quickly and well. We're not suggesting that creating a climate of imminent danger is a good motivational tool, but it does say something about the importance of relevance. Although the language purpose in the chemistry example is not as dramatic as a smoke-filled airplane cabin, knowing that you're going to develop a graphic organizer makes learning about halogens more relevant.

A second facet of motivation concerns competence. Learners are more motivated when they see themselves as capable learners. We've all witnessed the slouched shoulders of the student who has already decided that he or she won't do well in a subject. "I just can't do math," a student might say, "I'm not any good at it." This self-fulfilling prophecy is set into motion, and chances are very, very good that he or she will in fact not do well in math. Subsequently, the resulting lack of achievement in math is used as further evidence that he or she can't do math. It's a chain that is difficult to disrupt. This student is displaying a fixed view of intelligence that prevents him or her from doing well.

Unfortunately, this is sometimes unintentionally reinforced by well-meaning adults who praise intelligence ("You're so smart at this!") instead of effort ("I can see you worked hard on this!"). The difference is important because the latter focuses on a growth mind-set about intelligence (Dweck, 2007). Even among students who do well, praise about one's intelligence sets them up for failure because the only way they can interpret future difficulty in a subject is telling themselves they're *not* smart. In addition, these students limit the amount of educational challenge they are willing to assume because it might expose a lack of intelligence. Students who have been praised for their intelligence are less willing to try tasks at which they might not succeed because their belief is built around being viewed as intelligent (Dweck, 2007).

A fixed view of intelligence can also result in negative behavior. Learners who believe they don't do well because they're not smart are left with two undesirable choices—tell themselves either they're dumb or they're not doing well because they don't do the work. The second choice is the more desirable of the two because it preserves some scrap of self-concept. Follow the logic: "I'd rather be seen as lazy than dumb." The resultant work completion and attendance problems become predictable.

Students who correctly view intelligence as malleable understand that effort matters, recognize that not everything comes easily the first time around, and seek challenge because it means they are learning. They see learning as analogous to a muscle that needs to be flexed and exercised. Although they may suffer setbacks, they are more resilient because they know that their use of learning strategies—such as meeting with the teacher, asking questions, getting homework help, and studying for exams—will lead to improved performance. Students who are recognized for their efforts are more likely to develop this malleable growth mind-set.

It is wonderful when students arrive at our classroom doors with this mind-set, but the reality is that many don't. At our high school, we've made this topic a focal point throughout the school. During the first week of classes, students learn about persistence and a malleable view of intelligence. They take a 17-item questionnaire that measures "grit"—one's persistence and passion for long-term goals—in order to learn about themselves. Interestingly, grit has been found to be a primary factor in National Spelling Bee finalists, West Point graduates, and successful teachers (Duckworth, Petersen, Matthews, & Kelly, 2007). (This questionnaire, developed by Duckworth and her colleagues, can be downloaded at www.sas.upenn.edu/~duckwort/images/17-item%20Grit%20and%20Ambition.040709.pdf.)

Throughout the year, our students participate in lessons about brain physiology, intelligence, and learning theory, with special emphasis on a growth mind-set. We reinforce this by repeating one of the founding principles of our school—"It's never too late to learn." All of this would be pointless without student resources for changing their mind-sets. For this reason, we offer lunchtime and after-school tutorials, and every teacher holds office hours and schedules a weekly "academic recovery" for students who are falling behind. In addition, we have developed a grading system that replaces *D*s and *F*s with

Incomplete. This approach puts persistence into operation because students are required to make up missing or failed tests and assignments. Students who have carried an *Incomplete* for more than two weeks are put under contract and supported (some might say harassed) by a teacher who has been assigned full-time to the coordination of these efforts. The contract includes the student's plan for clearing any missing or failing assignments (see Figures 2.3 and 2.4). Any incomplete work at the end of the school year becomes their summer school curriculum (Fisher, Frey, & Grant, 2009). Students regularly receive handwritten "grit letters" addressed to them and mailed to their homes, congratulating them on their hard work and effort in the face of difficulties. These, along with similar notes congratulating those who do well in their classes, always focus on the role of effort—and not innate intelligence—as the variable responsible for their success. Families regularly tell us how much it means to their children to receive these cards in the mail.

The use of external motivation tools such as personal accountability, concrete and realistic plans for students who have fallen behind, and congratulatory notes are very different from the traditional extrinsic reward systems that rely on points and prizes. Rather, these motivational tools are intended to build a learner's capacity to develop intrinsic motivation skills that make it possible for the student to self-regulate. It's important to keep the learner's developmental level in mind as well. Obviously, an academic recovery plan isn't appropriate for a kindergarten student, but when the going gets tough, positive notes about hard work and family conferences are useful. The urge to give up often isn't due to lack of motivation but because the problem is perceived as being too complex to repair.

The process of developing and executing plans is in itself a rewarding experience, as it cultivates a sense of accomplishment. In addition, it fosters the ability to judge one's own progress toward a goal. In encouraging a growth mind-set, we hope to increase students' mastery of content and progress toward goals, with an emphasis on learning, while minimizing avoidance goals that focus on negative outcomes, which are often built on a fear of failure. These avoidance goals can be a manifestation of a fixed mind-set of intelligence.

Figure 2.3 | **Academic Recovery Contract**

ACADEMIC RECOVERY CHECKLIST

STUDENT NAME: _____

DATE OF CONFERENCE: _____

COURSE(S):
☐ Algebra I   ☐ Geometry   ☐ Algebra II

☐ World History   ☐ US History   ☐ Government

☐ English 9   ☐ English 10   ☐ English 11   ☐ English 12

☐ Earth Science   ☐ Biology   ☐ Physics   ☐ Integrated Science

☐ Health (Community College coursework)

☐ Other (specify) _____

Concerns:

The student will

☐ Enter assignments into the agenda at each class meeting.

☐ Find an assignment partner and exchange numbers for information or clarification.

☐ Have a separate folder for each class.

☐ Have a daily progress report signed.

☐ Have a weekly progress report signed.

☐ Print grades from Power School and return them to the teacher with a parent's signature each week.

☐ See an administrator (how often): _____

☐ Meet with the teacher during lunch every **M T W Th F** at _____ (circle all that apply).

The parent/guardian will

☐ Provide a consistent and quiet place to do homework.

☐ Provide encouragement, motivation, and prompting.

☐ Provide reasonable time expectations.

The teacher/school will

☐ Post assignments online and in class.

☐ Return corrected work to the student's mailbox in a timely fashion.

☐ Provide missing assignments.

☐ Initiate another student conference if progress is not seen.

☐ Initiate a family conference if progress is not seen.

_____	_____	_____
Student Signature	Parent Signature	Date
_____	_____	_____
Teacher Signature	Teacher Signature	Teacher Signature

Figure 2.4 | Student Plan for Academic Recovery

MY PLAN FOR ACADEMIC RECOVERY

What assignments are missing?	Targeted Date for Completion

What help do I need in order to be successful?	Who can help me?	Date

How will I know if I am being successful?

What is the first step to achieve my goal of academic recovery?

Setting Goals

Goals are closely linked to motivation, as they are key to putting a plan into action. However, the intent of the goals can shed insight into what motivates the student, and this can be useful knowledge for the teacher, school, and family. Goals are typically described in terms of mastery (learning) and performance (outcomes). These can be further expressed as approach (positive) and avoidance (negative) goals (see Figure 2.5). Learners with approach-oriented goals are attempting to move toward something, expressing a hope for success, whereas those with avoidance-oriented goals are expressing a fear of failure. Although fear of failure can certainly be motivating, the danger is that it can limit the learner's willingness to take an academic risk by assuming more challenging tasks.

Broadly speaking, young children in the primary grades appear to have an internal goal orientation based on past performance. If they have been successful reading one book, for example, they are likely to believe that they will do equally well with another. Why is this so? One theory is that they have not yet acquired a track record of failures and therefore don't have much reason to believe they won't do well (Harter, 1998). In addition, the social outlook of young children is directed toward the caring adults in their lives, especially parents and teachers. Their desire to do well in the eyes of these adults is a source of motivation and directs their goal-setting. Positive praise focused on effort is effective for young students, as is setting goals built on previous successes.

Figure 2.5	**Approach and Avoidance in Goal Setting**		
	Approach	**Avoidance**
Mastery	Write a research report on amphibians.	Get a better grade than I got on my last research report.
Performance	Earn a final grade of *A* in World History.	Pass World History so I won't flunk 10th grade.

As students enter the intermediate grades, their social orientation begins to shift from adults to peers. Children as young as 10 express curiosity about how others do on a task and how their peers' performances compare with their own (Bong, 2008). This is also a time when statements such as "I'm worried that I'm not smart/that I'll fail/that people won't like me" can begin to creep in. Though this is to be expected at this stage of development, this reaction signals the beginning of a belief that intelligence is fixed—which can lead to a diminished sense of control over one's own learning and achievement. This is a very real caution against displaying classwide achievement levels for students to view, as the results are damaging for children who are gauging their self-efficacy against others' performance.

At the same time, older students (especially those in middle school) are at risk for further paralysis as they begin to factor their own levels of effort in relation to achievement. Interestingly, this is the point at which higher-achieving students become at risk. Perceptions that they expended little effort and still managed a high level of achievement reinforce an innate sense of intelligence. As curriculum demands accelerate in high school, these students may feel as though their best days are behind them and that they are not smart enough to learn demanding content.

Students in middle school and high school are prime candidates for establishing challenge and commitment goals to minimize fear of failure while encouraging approach-oriented goals. Challenge goals require students to attain a measure of success that they have not yet experienced. For example, they might need to

- Earn an *A* on the next English test.
- Be able to name and identify the major bones in the human body.
- Solve 95 percent of the quadratic equations in Chapter 4 correctly.
- Identify the location of at least 80 countries on a world map.
- Master the forehand and backhand returns in tennis.

Commitment goals are used in addition to the challenge goals that students set for themselves. These goals focus on the effort and intermediate actions students will take to achieve the challenge goal. This type of goal is critical to attain the desired outcome, as it puts a plan into place. Even though the plan may change in the interim, it serves as a valid and helpful starting point. Some examples of commitment goals include

- Study nightly for each section of the English test.
- Use anatomy flash cards to test myself on the names of the bones at least twice a day.
- Meet with my math teacher at lunch and after school on Monday and Thursday.
- Practice locating countries on a virtual map.
- Use the tennis pitching machine to hit 100 tennis balls every day until the next match.

Even for younger students, challenge and commitment goals serve to develop a growing sense of self-efficacy. The youngest students may select one of a choice of three goals for the day, such as "I will read *The Hungry Caterpillar* with a friend today." Elementary students can develop goals in a journal and then refer back to them to self-assess. Over time, they internalize goal-setting and begin to internally regulate their actions toward those goals.

For instance, students can measure their progress in writing fluency by keeping a graph in their writing notebooks of the number of words they write each day during brief timed writing exercises called Power Writing (Frey & Fisher, 2006). For example, Tino, at the start of 4th grade, wrote 32 words per minute on average. He set a goal to write 40 words per minute on topic. Over time, Tino viewed his own progress and saw how he was progressing toward his personal challenge goal. Soon, Tino was regularly writing 40 words per minute and then increased his goal to 45 words per minute with a reduced number of errors.

The overarching purpose for establishing goals with learners is to develop their ability to self-regulate behaviors and attitudes. Self-regulation represents a coordination of the elements discussed in this chapter, especially leveraging motivation to set a goal, pursuing it through the use of strategic actions, and reflecting on the extent to which the goal was met, how it was accomplished, and what should be done next (Zimmerman, 1990). It's a tall order, and fully self-regulated behavior doesn't occur until adulthood—indeed, more than anything else, it is what many of us would use as a defining characteristic of mature adulthood. However, the ability to self-regulate doesn't suddenly occur. It is fostered throughout a student's educational career and begins the day he or she arrives at the classroom door. In later chapters, we will continue to discuss self-regulation as a major outcome in a sophisticated formative assessment system.

Making It All Possible

Many of the factors we have discussed in this chapter are internal to the learner. We can set aside time in our day to write objectives and set purposes, and we can even develop schoolwide processes intended to foster motivation, but goals and purposes are meaningless if they are pursued only for compliance.

This is the difficulty of influencing learners' internal motivational factors in a positive way; they are not strictly behavioral in nature. For instance, a student probably isn't going to tell you that her real goal is to avoid looking like a loser to her friends. Nor is a student with a behavior problem going to let you know that he's misbehaving because his mind-set is that intelligence is fixed and he's not sure he can ever learn how to spell well. Motivation and goal-setting involve emotional and psychological elements as much as they do outward behaviors. The most confusing part (for teachers) is that outward behaviors can manifest internal emotions.

We can't just throw up our hands and disregard these internal functions—we've come too far in our understanding of learning to do that. We can, however, indirectly influence motivation and goal-setting so that students move in a positive direction. The good news is that these teacher-based influences are well known in education. They involve choice and differentiation.

Use Choice to Motivate

The importance of choice cannot be overestimated for even the youngest of learners. Primary teachers typically offer several tasks to be completed, but they allow choice about the order in which students will do them. Older students in effective classrooms experience even more choice as they select topics of study, identify partners to work with, or pick from a menu of possible ways to exhibit their mastery of a subject. One teacher we know has a list of possible ways to demonstrate knowledge—from essays to posters to poems to tests—and students select the form of their demonstration for each unit of study. The choices provided must be viewed as relevant, but in the best of situations, choice breeds autonomy when it is aligned to a learner's goals and areas of interest.

Reading selections is one area where choice is especially important. Assigned texts reduce choice and often serve to reduce motivation. When students are told that they *must* read a specific book, they often search for summary materials so they can complete assignments. As a result, they read less, even though we know that reading builds background knowledge and vocabulary (Nagy, Anderson, & Herman, 1987). Instead, teachers should set a purpose for reading and then help students choose material to read that will meet that purpose. They can read the same text while they are in class working with peers but choose other texts to read on their own time. For example, we organize our curriculum around essential questions and then identify a wide range of reading materials that students can choose. The books have different difficulty levels, represent diverse perspectives, and provide students with things to think about relative to the essential question. Students report reading more than ever, liking what they read, and performing better on summative tests (Frey, Fisher, & Moore, 2009). Consider the essential question "Does age matter?" To support this question, students could choose from more than 50 titles, including

- *Hitler Youth: Growing Up in Hitler's Shadow*, by Susan Campbell Bartoletti
- *The Last Lecture*, by Randy Pausch
- *Tuck Everlasting*, by Natalie Babbitt
- *Pride and Prejudice*, by Jane Austen
- *The Secret Life of Bees*, by Sue Monk Kidd

In addition to completing learning tasks, choice is an important factor in setting goals. To be sure, teachers can and should provide guidance on the development of goals, especially in moving students from avoidance goals to approach-oriented ones. However, there is a limit to the level of control one should exert on an individual's goals—too much control, and the goals have become yours, not the student's. In cases where the goals seem to be less than helpful ("I want to go to the moon" or "I want to not get yelled at today"), then goal-setting can be a co-constructed activity. In the school district where we teach, principals and teachers work together to develop three goals for evaluation. The teacher identifies the first goal, and the second comes from the administrator. The third is jointly negotiated and developed. In the same way, goals for individual students can be written together so that the student learns how to set meaningful goals while also maintaining a sense of choice about them.

Motivate with Differentiation

Another way we can motivate students is through differentiation. Carol Ann Tomlinson (2001) notes that teachers can differentiate content, process, or product. In doing so, the teacher provides students with materials or a task that is challenging but not frustrating, which is in and of itself motivating. Differentiation is motivating on several other levels as well. When a teacher says, "I saw this book and thought of you," the rapport between student and teacher strengthens, and the student knows he or she is cared about. That's pretty motivating. In addition, when the product has been differentiated so the student tries hard and experiences success, motivation increases. Of course, there is a potential pitfall: If only a few students receive "differentiated stuff," they will begin to compare their work with others in the class and begin to doubt their success and think they aren't smart. Differentiation must be the standard operating system, rather than a special procedure used when all else fails.

In Ms. Baldwin's class, students understand the purpose of each lesson and know that their work may differ daily from that of other students in the class. While they were studying "People Who Make a Difference," for example, each student selected a person of interest and worked with the librarian to locate information about that person. Students had a choice of products they could create—a report, a skit, a poem, a rap—and met with Ms. Baldwin in small groups to receive feedback on their projects as they developed. Ms. Baldwin also selected a person to research and demonstrated her learning alongside her students. As she noted errors or misconceptions in the group, she addressed them through her own study of George Washington Carver. Ms. Baldwin's product was a picture book that she produced using an online photo service. She decided to do this because none of the other students had selected this option, and she wanted to show them that there were a number of different ways to demonstrate learning. She found a number of public domain pictures available online that she could use without violating copyright and wrote her own text about the "Peanut Man." Students in Ms. Baldwin's class completed their projects because they were motivated to do so. This motivation came, in part, because Ms. Baldwin differentiated her curriculum and instruction.

Looking Back, Looking Forward

In this chapter, we've focused on the first part of the formative assessment process: feed-up. As we have noted, students deserve to know the purpose of each lesson and why that information is important and relevant. In addition, we've explored the role of motivation. Interestingly, a fixed mind-set about intelligence can be harmful for students, and praise about their intelligence can work against them. As educators, we have to help students see intelligence as malleable and recognize their efforts to master learning. Goal-setting is another area that is important in the feed-up process. There are different types of goals, but orienting students toward their goals helps them achieve more. When purpose is aligned with goals, and students are motivated, the formative assessment system is in motion. With these conditions present, the student performance data we collect will represent students' best efforts and guide our instruction.

Once goals are agreed upon and instruction begins, the teacher must check for understanding to determine if students are making progress toward their goals. In the next chapter, we turn our attention to the various ways teachers can determine what students understand and what is still unclear.

3

Checking for Understanding: Where Am I Now?

"Any questions?" No response from the students.

"Okay, then, everybody's got that, right?" Again, no response.

"Okay, then, let's post our comments on this thread. Remember that we can use voice or text."

Suddenly hands go up everywhere. One student asks, "Can you come here and help me?" Another asks, "How do I get to that page?" A third asks, "Where's the microphone button?"

The teacher scurries around the room providing individual help to the students, meeting as many of their needs as possible, given the time constraints. The teacher finishes the class exhausted, knowing that most students did not meet their goals.

This did not happen in an elementary or secondary classroom but, rather, with a group of teachers in a technology seminar—teachers such as Nancy who are very interested in Web 2.0 applications and figuring out the latest interaction tools. These teachers attend seminars and training classes, both live and virtual, to extend their knowledge. In the seminar described above, Nancy's purpose was to learn about VoiceThread and other interactive tools. She did increase her knowledge of technology, but she also was reminded that learners simply don't respond well to generic checking-for-understanding efforts and that a failure to adequately check for understanding often results in exhausted teachers and frustrated students.

As a learner, Nancy experienced that frustration. It is true that she didn't respond to the teacher's generic efforts to check for understanding, but that was because she didn't know what she didn't know. Instead, she wished the teacher had planned some formative assessments to determine what she knew and what she still needed to learn. This information would have allowed her to determine an answer to the question "Where am I going next?"

That's why checking for understanding must occur simultaneously with instruction, rather than after instruction has been given. Once the purpose has been established and instruction has begun, the teacher must continuously monitor students' understanding.

Here's where formative assessment takes on a new dimension. It shouldn't *just* be about how the teacher discovers what the learners know; the daily application of formative assessment techniques should also foster each student's capacity to assess himself or herself. In the same way that students need to be kept at the center of the processes to establish purpose, build motivation, and set goals, so should they be at the core of what occurs during formative assessments.

Keeping Students at the Center of Formative Assessment

In some quarters, formative assessment has become more formal and held apart from the daily instructional flow. We acknowledge the usefulness of benchmark assessments and the productive conversations that can happen when teachers discuss student learning. However, many of these "formalized" assessments have taken on a quasi-summative feel. Benchmark assessments are often administered at scheduled intervals throughout the year using published, rather than teacher-created, materials. This approach can certainly smooth some of the rough edges regarding needs assessment and accountability, but the trade-off is that the information assessed may come too early or too late in the instructional cycle.

In the absence of effective techniques for monitoring student understanding throughout a lesson, learning suffers. To be sure, students who are struggling academically are much less likely to ask a question than those students who are doing well (Nelson-Le Gall, 1985). This reluctance to ask questions may be due to social reasons—particularly an unwillingness to expose a lack of understanding to classmates and teachers—yet it may also occur because students simply don't know enough about a topic in order to ask a relevant question.

The teacher's role in daily formative assessments should be active, and it should overlap with many other markers of active teacher involvement, including a sensitivity to student needs, emotional and instructional supports, and high-quality feedback given to struggling students (Pianta, LaParo, & Hamre, 2008). Together, these behaviors suggest that the teacher views learning as interactive and that monitoring student understanding is essential to teaching. Numerous other researchers report similar findings as a hallmark of effective teaching (e.g., Emmer & Evertson, 2008; Good & Brophy, 2007; Stronge, 2007).

A student-centered approach to formative assessment is a dynamic one. Most teachers learn early in their careers that daily lesson plans can capture only the most obvious details of a learning event. No amount of planning could possibly allow for what actually happens when student understanding either bogs down or suddenly advances.

Good planning requires incorporating a variety of ways to check for understanding—and then implementing these checks *as instruction is being given*. Without this focus, the benefit of the instruction is diminished. Research into the differences between observations made by expert and novice teachers during certain lessons revealed that experts noticed more details, especially when student assistance was needed to clarify understanding (Krull, Oras, & Sisack, 2007). This may be due in part to expert teachers' trained ability to recall events, which allows them to view learning in chunks rather than as discrete events (Ross & Gibson, 2010). However, the role of building each other's capacity for noticing student learning is usually overlooked in many formative assessment systems, where the data take precedence over the gathering techniques.

The remainder of this chapter is devoted to a number of instructional techniques that can be used effectively to check for understanding. We will focus on oral language, writing, projects and performances, tests, and common assessments. Although techniques can be described and illustrated, the way that experts notice student learning cannot be directly explained, unfortunately. Among colleagues, conversation about expert-level observations should be an inherent part of the formative assessment process. More information and further examples can be found in *Checking for Understanding: Formative Assessment Techniques for Your Classroom* (Fisher & Frey, 2007a).

Using Oral Language to Check for Understanding

One of the most common ways that we, as teachers, can check for understanding is through oral language. When students talk—and we listen—we can get a sense of what they understand and what they still need to learn. It's important to remember that several language functions are required of students in school. Carl Bereiter and Siegfried Engelmann (cited in Justice, 2006, p. 72) identified 10 language functions that still serve as a useful organizational system:

1. *To instruct:* To provide specific sequential directions.
2. *To inquire:* To seek understanding through asking questions.
3. *To test:* To investigate the logic of a statement.
4. *To describe:* To tell about giving necessary information to identify.
5. *To compare and contrast:* To show how things are similar and different.
6. *To explain:* To define terms by providing specific examples.
7. *To analyze:* To break down a statement into its component parts, tell what each means, and show how they are related.
8. *To hypothesize:* To test a statement's logical or empirical consequences.
9. *To deduce:* To arrive at a conclusion by reasoning; to infer.
10. *To evaluate:* To weigh and judge the relative importance of an idea.

There are a number of ways to use language to check for understanding, and we will provide examples of some of them here.

Questioning

Arguably, the most common way that teachers use oral language to check for understanding is through questioning. There are good—and not so good—ways to use oral questions.

One not-so-good way is known as the Initiate-Respond-Evaluate (IRE) model of questioning, which unfortunately dominates classroom discourse (e.g., Cazden, 1988). In this model, the teacher asks a question, specific students are called on to answer the question, and the teacher evaluates the responses. A typical interaction might sound something like this:

Teacher: What is the moral of this story?
Student 1: That "good" eventually wins over "bad."
Teacher: Right, and how is that different from a theme?
Student 2: The theme is broader. It's the whole story, not just what one reader learned.
Teacher: Yes. Are there any other differences between a theme and a moral?

As is typical in IRE discussions, only one student talks at a time and tries to guess what is in the teacher's mind. The students all know that the teacher knows the answer, and yet they play along, humoring the teacher for some reason: typically grades, fear, or interest. What doesn't happen in the IRE model is checking the understanding of all students.

Questions must be posed so students struggle with their responses. They should have opportunities to talk with others around them about their answers, and they should also generate their own questions. We have already presented Bloom's taxonomy and its 21st-century revision (in Chapter 1), but consider the types of questions that can be asked using that framework.

• *Remembering:* What happened in the last act of the play—*Our Town*—that we're reading?

• *Understanding:* Why do you think the playwright has the stage manager step into the action?

• *Applying:* At the end of the play, Emily says, "Oh, Earth, you're too wonderful for anybody to realize you. Do any human beings ever realize life while they live it?" Which "wonderful" things about Earth and life do you fail to notice?

• *Analyzing:* In what ways is our town like Grover's Corners?

• *Evaluating:* If you were to make a movie based on *Our Town*, would you include elaborate sets or retain the spare sets, with few props?

• *Creating:* Is the symbolism—the trains, the tombstones, and the stage manager's watch—effective to show the passage of time? What other symbols could be used to denote the passage of time?

These questions can really get students talking since they don't have clearly defined, "correct" answers. There may be some wrong answers, but there will be a whole bunch of right ones. As students interact with one another and figure out what they think, the teacher listens and identifies areas of understanding and areas in need of additional instruction.

Retelling

Retellings allow students to consider information and then orally summarize what they understand about that information. Retellings require students to process information, thinking about the sequence of ideas and events and their relative importance. Inviting students to retell what they have just heard or read is a powerful way to check understanding (Shaw, 2005). In fact, retellings can be more effective in checking for understanding than direct questioning (Gambrell, Koskinen, & Kapinus, 1991).

To introduce retelling, teachers should

1. Explain that the purpose of a retelling is to re-create the information in your own words.

2. Ask students to discuss the ways in which they talk about their favorite movie or song.

3. Make the connection between talking about a movie or song and talking about other types of information.

4. Model a retelling from a short piece of familiar text, which allows students to compare the original with the retelling.

5. Ask students to discuss the similarities and differences between the original and the retelling.

6. Select a new piece of text, read it aloud, and have the class create a retelling as a group.

As students become increasingly familiar with retellings, they can be used regularly and even assessed formally. A number of rubrics for retellings are available on the Internet, each representing specific components or areas of emphasis. There are retelling rubrics for informational texts, as well as rubrics specific to math, science, social studies, and art. Teachers who use retellings to check for understanding of narrative texts can look for the following characteristics:

- The student correctly sequences major events into "beginning," "middle," and "end."
- The student describes the setting and plot in detail.
- The student identifies and elaborates on main characters.
- The student identifies and elaborates upon the problem, conflict, or quest and its resolution.

In her math class, Ms. Wheaton has a significant portion of the wall devoted to the components of the retelling process as they relate to mathematical problem-solving processes (see Figure 3.1). The students in Ms. Wheaton's prealgebra class know that they are expected to retell how they solve problems so their teacher can understand their thinking and how to help them, if they need it. Wendy, a student in Ms. Wheaton's class, retold how she solved the following problem: *The original price of a microphone: $129.99. The tax is 7%. What is the total price you have to pay for this microphone?* Wendy's retelling included the following description:

> So, the problem is asking me how much I have to pay for this mic. The information I know is the price and how much tax they make you pay. I think it has to be more than $129, like maybe $150, because the tax is on top of the price. I have to add the tax to the price. But I have to find out how much the tax is. I think you multiply. So I did $129.99 times 7, but that is $909 and that is too much for the microphone. The answer isn't reasonable. But I don't know why it didn't work.

This simple task gave Ms. Wheaton all of the information she needed to help Wendy. Wendy knew she was stuck, but she didn't know what to do next. (We'll save the feedback and feed-forward conversation for later in this book. For now, it's important to focus on determining what students understand and still need to be taught.) It's not the case that Wendy knew nothing about this type of problem; rather, she understood much but made a mistake in a specific aspect of the problem.

Figure 3.1 | **Math Retelling Components**

1. Identify what the problem is asking.

2. Locate relevant and irrelevant information.

3. Estimate the answer.

4. Define the procedure.

5. Follow the sequence of the procedure.

6. Describe problem-solving steps.

7. Identify the answer and decide if that answer is reasonable.

Think-Pair-Share

Think-Pair-Share is a cooperative discussion strategy that allows students to discuss their responses with a peer before sharing their ideas with the whole class. Developed by Frank Lyman (1981) and his colleagues, the strategy has three stages of student action:

1. *Think.* The teacher engages students' thinking with a question, prompt, reading, visual, or observation. The students take a few moments (not minutes) just to THINK about the question.

2. *Pair.* Using designated partners, students PAIR up to discuss their respective responses. They compare their thoughts and identify the responses they think are the best, most intriguing, most convincing, or most creative.

3. *Share.* After students talk in pairs for a few moments, the teacher asks pairs to SHARE their thinking with the rest of the class.

This activity offers great opportunities to check for understanding. The teacher can listen as pairs of students discuss their responses and note how responses are being shared. For example, Mr. Dexter listened to pairs of students discussing the Zimmerman Telegram. This 1917 telegram, written in code, was from Germany to Mexico and encouraged Mexico to go to war against the United States if it did not remain neutral. Mexico ignored the telegram, but it angered the American people and contributed to the country entering the war. Listening to his students as they read and discussed the telegram, Mr. Dexter knew that they were still confused. This is an example of what he heard:

> **Sean**: I think that this says that they want America to stay out of the war.
> **Alexis**: Yeah, but it says that they're gonna start submarine warfare on February 1.
> **Sean**: So America should have stayed out.
> **Alexis**: But they are threatening the whole world. They're talking about Mexico, the United States, and Japan.
> **Sean**: But the United States wouldn't fight Mexico. I'm confused.

Mr. Dexter knew, from listening to Sean, Alexis, and several other groups, that they needed a better historical context and that the students were thinking about the world today and not the world of 1917. As a result, he decided to build their background knowledge and then return to this important document to push their thinking further.

Using Writing to Check for Understanding

Writing is a complex cognitive process that obviously involves thinking. In fact, it's hard to do anything but think while you write. As such, writing provides an interesting glimpse of how students think.

Nevertheless, writing is more than thinking. It's not as simple as saying that you write what you think. Instead, you think as you write. You clarify your understanding as you write. You learn as you write. That's part of the power of using writing to check for understanding: Teachers get to see how students think, and students get to clarify their understanding.

Consider the following excerpt from an essay that a student gave to Nancy. This excerpt gave Nancy an interesting glimpse of how this difficult student perceived herself, and it helped Nancy identify support strategies to make her successful.

> On the inside I am not like everyone else. I hide most of my emotions because I do not want people to know how I feel. I think if people knew my secrets they would use it against me. I have been made to feel dumb, because people have

told me I am. Being called dumb makes me feel mad. In general I am an angry person, I think this is because when I was young my father left my family. I think I take this pain out on other people in my life. I feel as if I am treated differently, other people can do no wrong and anything I do I get into trouble for.

The kind of writing that facilitates checking for understanding is not the "process writing" assigned by English teachers. (Of course, English teachers can use process writing to check students' understanding on the standards they're teaching—but that won't work for teachers of other subjects.) We're talking about two different types of writing, each with separate goals.

> It is helpful to distinguish between two very different goals for writing. The normal and conventional goal is writing to demonstrate learning: for this goal the writing should be good—it should be clear and, well . . . right. It is high stakes writing. We all know and value this kind of writing so I don't need to argue for it here, but let me give one more reason why it's important: If we don't ask students to demonstrate their learning in essays and essay exams, we are likely to grade unfairly because of being misled about how much they have learned in our course. For students often seem to know things on short-answer or multiple-choice tests that they don't really understand.
>
> But there is another important kind of writing that is less commonly used and valued, and so I want to stress it here: writing for learning. This is low-stakes writing. The goal isn't so much good writing as coming to learn, understand, remember and figure out what you don't yet know. Even though low-stakes writing-to-learn is not always good . . . writing, it is particularly effective at promoting learning and involvement in course material, and it is much easier on teachers—especially those who aren't writing teachers. (Elbow, 1994, p. 1)

It is this second kind of writing—writing for learning—that is used to check understanding. Here are some writing tasks that teachers use to determine "next steps" or feed-forward instruction.

Summary Writing

Summary writing is a valuable tool for checking for understanding because it provides the teacher with insight into how students condense information. It is similar to retelling in that it serves as a way for students to demonstrate their ability to synthesize what they have read, viewed, or done.

The most common form of summary writing is the précis, a short piece that contains the major ideas or concepts of a topic. The emphasis is on an economy of words and an accurate rendering of the read or observed phenomena. Before summaries are useful in checking for understanding, though, students must be taught how to summarize. Too often, student "summaries" are longer than the original text and use too many of the author's words. There are a number of ways to teach summary writing, but we have experienced the most success with the Generating Interaction Between Schemata and Text (GIST) model. These are the steps in teaching students to summarize using GIST (adapted from Frey, Fisher, & Hernandez, 2003):

1. Distribute copies of a short text. Each text should be divided into four or five sections that represent logical summarizing points, indicated by a line and the word *STOP* in the margin.

2. Explain the GIST process. Students should read a portion of a text, stop, and then write a sentence that summarizes the general idea—or gist—of the passage. At the end of the text, students will have written four or five sentences, or a concise summary of the text.

3. Introduce the text to be read, build prior knowledge, and discuss key vocabulary. Read aloud the first passage of the text while students read along silently.

4. Lead a class discussion about important facts from the passage. Write students' ideas, questions, and contributions on the board.

5. Lead a class discussion about how to formulate ideas into a sentence. Allow students to share ideas and negotiate those ideas to craft an accurate and precise sentence.

6. Write the agreed-upon sentence on the board. Label the sentence as #1 and have students write it in their journals.

7. Read the second passage aloud. Follow the same sequence above, and label the agreed-upon sentence as #2. Repeat this cycle until you are finished with the text.

8. Discuss how the class has condensed a page of text into a limited number of sentences. Reread the series of sentences to check for meaning. Make any changes necessary so that it serves as a concise written summary.

A rubric useful in evaluating summaries can be found in Figure 3.2.

Figure 3.2	**Rubric for Assessing Summary Writing**			
	4	**3**	**2**	**1**
Length	**6–8 sentences**	**9 sentences**	**10 sentences**	**11+ sentences**
Accuracy	All statements are accurate and verified in the text.	Most statements are accurate and verified.	Some statements cite outside information or opinions.	Most statements cite outside information or opinions.
Paraphrasing	No more than four words in a row are taken directly from the text.	One sentence contains more than four words in a row taken directly from the text.	Two sentences contain more than four words in a row taken directly from the text.	Three or more sentences contain more than four words in a row taken directly from the text.
Focus	Summary consists of main idea and important details only.	Summary contains main idea and some minor details.	Summary contains main idea and only minor details.	Main idea is not discussed.
Conventions	No more than one punctuation, grammar, or spelling error.	Two to three punctuation, grammar, or spelling errors.	Four to five punctuation, grammar, or spelling errors.	Six or more punctuation, grammar, or spelling errors.

Source: From "What's the gist? Summary writing for struggling adolescent writers," by N. Frey, D. Fisher, and T. Hernandez, 2003, *Voices from the Middle, 11*(2), p. 48. Copyright 2003 by the National Council of Teachers of English. Adapted with permission.

Writing Prompts

Many writing prompts can be useful in checking for understanding. For example, consider exit slips, used for "closure" activities. Students write on a topic or question that the teacher supplies, and they hand the paper to their teacher on their way out of class. The teacher then reviews the exit slips for content information, making decisions about what students understand and what they still need to be taught. For example, a prompt for biology might read, "Describe the similarities and differences between zooplankton and protoplankton." A social studies prompt that is part of a unit on westward expansion might be "Would you have gone in the covered wagon? Why, or why not?" Other helpful writing prompts include the following (Fisher & Frey, 2008b):

• *Admit Slips:* Upon entering the classroom, students write on an assigned topic such as "Who was Churchill, and why should we care?" or "Describe the process of cell division."

• *Crystal Ball:* Students describe what they think class will be about, what might happen next in the novel they're reading, or the next step in a science lab.

• *Found Poems:* Students reread a piece of text, either something they have written or something published, and find key phrases. They arrange these into a poem without adding any new words.

• *Awards:* Students recommend someone or something for an award that the teacher has created, such as "Most Interesting Character" or "Most Dangerous Chemical."

• *Yesterday's News:* Students summarize the information presented the day before, from either a film, lecture, discussion, or reading.

• *Take a Stand:* Students discuss their opinions about a controversial topic such as "What is race, and does it matter?" or "What's worth dying for?"

• *Letters:* Students write letters to others, including elected officials, family members, friends, or people who have made a difference. For example, students may respond to the prompt "Write to Martin Luther King Jr. about the progress that has, or has not, been made related to civil rights."

As an example of the power of writing prompts used to check for understanding, read the following response to a Crystal Ball prompt given when students were about halfway through the book *Charlotte's Web*:

I think that Charlotte will save Wilbur, because it is a story and not real. He won't get eaten for dinner at Christmas. I think that she will have baby spiders and the whole family will get Wilbur out of the farm. Or maybe Fern will help Wilbur because she likes him a lot and can hear what he says. Because Wilbur is worried and Fern wants him to be safe.

It's obvious that this student understands the key idea of the text thus far and knows the characters and their likely actions. She also understands the difference between fiction and nonfiction and how stories work. This short writing sample demonstrates the thinking of an 8-year-old, including what she understands and still needs to be taught.

RAFT

Our experience suggests that RAFT writing-to-learn prompts are especially helpful in checking for understanding. RAFT writing prompts are designed to help students incorporate different perspectives into their writing (Santa & Havens, 1995). RAFT prompts provide a scaffold for students as they explore writing by taking on various roles, audiences, and formats (Fisher & Frey, 2007c). RAFT is an acronym for:

Role—What is the role of the writer?
Audience—To whom is the writer writing?
Format—What is the format for the writing?
Topic—What is the focus of the writing?

Here is one student's response to the RAFT prompt used in a unit exploring the essential question "Can you buy your way to happiness?"

R—a human being, maybe you
A—other humans
F—free verse poem
T—buying happiness

This student's poem expresses his unique understanding of the question as well as what he wants to share with his audience:

Money
People
Greedy heartbreakers
Can I have a quarter?
Get your own . . .
Our society
Crumbling . . . slowly
Is it us?
Or those surrounding us?
Life slowly turning in the dryer
Then
Silence
What is that coming in the dryer?
So soft and delicate
A little sheet of fabric softener called love
Is it here to help?
Or hurt?
I don't know but for some reason . . .
I feel . . . safe.

Using Projects and Performances to Check for Understanding

Much of the work that students do in classrooms focuses on the projects and performances that mark each unit. These are often seen primarily as capstone experiences designed to challenge learners to synthesize, evaluate, and create. Even though they are often featured near the end of the learning cycle, they can also be used as a means for formative assessment throughout the unit. Keep in mind that performance is not synonymous with a public display; performance is the execution of a skill or process.

Shadowing and Reiteration

A formative assessment technique that typically occurs early in a lesson is shadowing (Siedentop, 1991). This technique requires students to replicate a movement or skill so that the teacher can assess how closely they are approaching competence. A dance teacher, for example, demonstrates a series of steps and then breaks them into discrete movements as students mirror her. She rapidly scans the group and coaches individual students who are not yet fully executing the move. A mathematics teacher stops periodically while solving an equation and instructs her students to calculate the next step while she looks on to see if each is proceeding correctly. A kindergarten teacher writes the letter *B* on chart paper and invites his students to write the same letter on their response boards. As they do so, he quickly checks each for proper formation and orientation. Each of these is an example of using shadowing as a technique for early formative assessment.

A second related technique is reiteration (Rauschenbach, 1994). This can follow shadowing and involves students restating the concept or skill in their own words to a partner, usually accompanied by another demonstration. After shadowing the teacher in dance class, for instance, partners turn to one another and execute the same steps, repeating the oral directions as they go. In the mathematics class, students turn to one another to explain their answers and show how they solved the problem. In the kindergarten class, the teacher asks students to show one another their whiteboards. In each case, the teacher is circulating, listening, and watching for clues about each student's level of learning.

These simple ways to check for understanding represent small instructional moves that belie the sophisticated teaching behind them and represent the difference between a novice approach and an expert one. The novice views both shadowing and reiteration as a means to provide more practice since each requires the learner to mirror the teacher. However, in the hands of an expert, this is also an opportunity to gather formative assessment information in order to make an informed decision about what to do next. In other words, is more time spent reteaching required, or is it time to move on to the next skill?

Checklists During Projects

Most projects take a relatively long time to complete (often several class periods) and can quickly go astray if there is no method for checking progress. It can also be difficult for the teacher to manage so many projects in various states of preparation and completion. Deceptively simple, checklists are a great tool for keeping students on track and for checking their growing understanding of skills and concepts.

> In a complex environment, experts are up against two main difficulties. The first is the fallibility of human memory and attention, especially when it comes to mundane, routine matters that are easily overlooked under the strain of more pressing events . . . . A further difficulty, just as insidious, is that people can lull themselves into skipping steps even when they remember them. In complex processes, after all, certain steps don't *always* matter . . . . Checklists seem to provide protection against such failures. They remind us of the minimum necessary steps and make them explicit. (Gawande, 2009, p. 36)

Building a diorama of the Battle of Bunker Hill, for example, may not seem as complex as repairing a torn aorta, but to a learner unfamiliar with the material, it is—and that's the point. Projects are designed to give students the opportunity to synthesize what they have been learning in an effort to create something new, and they are not always especially effective at using background knowledge and newer concepts. Checklists keep students on track, and they also provide a means for teacher–student interaction during project development.

Checklists have been useful for Dr. Moore, a 9th grade English teacher. Dr. Moore's students write a letter to her each week about the text they're reading independently (Frey, Fisher, & Moore, 2009). This practice allows her to stay in communication with them about their reading. Because keeping track of 150 readings a week is difficult, Dr. Moore developed a checklist to accompany the weekly literacy letters (see Figure 3.3). The checklist that students use each week includes items that have become routine, such as underlining the title of the book, and some that are more complex, such as asking questions about how the story would be different if the main character were older or younger. The checklist gives Dr. Moore a way to check for understanding with her students before they finish the assignment. Consider the following exchange to see how this might play out.

Figure 3.3 | **Dr. Moore's Checklist**

Name *Amal*

Literacy Letter #15
checklist

Please turn in this checklist stapled to your literacy letter

☑ Font: Times New Roman, size 12

☑ Double spaced

☑ Title underlined?

☑ Include the author?

☑ Date written out: February 6, 2009

☑ Greeting with a comma: Dear Dr. Moore,

☑ Indent paragraph #1

☑ **Paragraph #1 (1/2 page): Write an update of your book.**

☑ Indent paragraph #2

☑ **Paragraph #2: Think about the main character in your book. How old is he/she? The author deliberately created this character to be this age. Why? How would the story be different if he/she was younger? Older?**

☑ Closing with a comma: Sincerely,

☑ Signature under the closing

☑ P.S. I rate my book a _____.

☑ Spell & grammar check?

☑ Read it once

☑ Reread it!

☑ Reread it aloud!

Dr. Moore: Amal, how are you doing on your literacy letter?

Amal: I think I'm doing OK.

Dr. Moore: Let me check to see what you've got so far. [Pauses to read letter.] You've got your opening formatted correctly [checks off items], and you've written a short update of your book so far. You're reading *Thirteen Reasons Why*. That's a pretty heavy topic. Why did you choose it?

Amal: Yeah, it's really sad. This girl, Hannah, she committed suicide and then left these tapes for people to listen to.

Dr. Moore: Wow . . . . What's your reaction so far? How come you chose this?

Amal: Well, I have an aunt who killed herself when I was little. I don't really remember much about her, but I see how much it still hurts my family that she did that. My mom especially.

Dr. Moore: I'm so sorry to hear that. The pain from that kind of loss probably never goes away. How old was she?

Amal: She was 21.

Dr. Moore: Older than Hannah, huh? Are you seeing parallels to your aunt, or is it different?

Amal: Well, some, but not a lot. Hannah seems so angry, like she wants to make sure everyone knows why she's gone. It's like it was more planned, and she wanted to make sure other people hurt, too. It wasn't like that with my aunt. She had clinical depression for years and it's almost like she slipped away. There wasn't this big production that she left behind.

Dr. Moore: You sound like you're angry with Hannah because of what she did.

Amal: I kinda am. Like bugged, more than angry. It just seems babyish, wanting to lash out like that.

Dr. Moore: So is any of that a function of age? Do any of those ideas belong in your second paragraph?

The conversation continued for a few minutes more, and Amal turned back to her letter with a new perspective on how she would approach the question. In this case, both the checklist and the interaction with the teacher spurred new learning to occur, as is often the case when checking for understanding.

Presentations

At some point, most teachers assign student-designed and student-led presentations about a topic studied in class. However, listeners can find them tedious, and teachers may eventually question whether much good arises from these presentations, which seem to feature questionable information, lots of reading directly from notes, and far too many PowerPoint slides! Still, students need opportunities to share information with peers so they can become stronger public speakers who can discuss ideas. Presentations can also be an excellent way to assess student knowledge about a topic, but it's difficult to make any corrections if the first time you've seen the presentation is when the student is standing in front of the class.

There are ways to structure presentations so that you can gather formative, not just summative, information. The availability of technology has made some of this information gathering much easier to accomplish today than it was even five years ago. For instance, 6th grade social studies teacher Mr. Billingsley has each of his students deliver a two-minute summary of the main points in front of a video camera as a way to prepare for the longer presentation due a few weeks later. He uploads these short videos to his school's e-platform and launches a monitored discussion board. Students choose three videos to watch and then leave their feedback on the discussion board. The students must summarize the speaker's main talking points as they understand them, give specific feedback on two effective behaviors the speaker uses to make his or her message understood, and make one suggestion for improvement. Comments about unrelated topics such as appearance are not allowed—comments must focus on the content of the ideas and the movement, gestures, and voice used by the speaker.

Mr. Billingsley has set up the discussion board so that he must approve the comments before they are posted for public view. "I've actually had to do very little correction in the two years I've been doing this," he remarks. "We spend a lot of time before this in talking about the ways we support one another. Anonymous comments are not allowed on the board, so there's a high degree of accountability to each other."

Watching each of the videos and reading his students' comments give Mr. Billingsley insight into what each speaker needs. "It helps me with follow-up because the kids are interested in improving," he says.

As another example, Ms. Alexander teaches 4th grade students, many of whom are English language learners. "I've become a big fan of student-made podcasts," she says. Indeed, the technology has become easier to access, and her students have become very adept at it. "One of the things I like about the podcasts is that they are easy to rerecord," she adds. "Some of my students are reluctant to speak in front of others, and this gives them a way to play back their podcast before posting it. If they don't like it, they delete it and do it again."

She also uses a collaborative presentation website called VoiceThread (www.voicethread.com) that allows students to upload presentation materials and either record or create text to accompany each slide. According to Ms. Alexander: "It's been great when they need visuals to accompany their speeches." In addition, subsequent viewers can also ask questions and pose additional comments on the slides. "I'm the first one to view it," she says. "Once they've got their draft presentation posted, I listen to it and do some initial assessment. I record further questions and suggestions for them so that they can make any changes necessary. Once they're ready, they open it up for the entire class to view."

Using Tests to Check for Understanding

Although tests are most commonly used as summative assessments, they can also be used in formative ways, such as when they are used as quizzes to check for understanding. A review on effective uses of testing reports that it "not only enhances learning but also slows the rate of forgetting" (Rohrer & Pashler, 2010, p. 406).

The issue of forgetting is not a small one, as newly learned material is more quickly forgotten if it is not used again within a short time. The forgetting curve is longer for more practiced skills, but those will also deteriorate over time if not used. There are a number of types of tests, some of which are described below.

Short Quizzes

These can be useful for promoting retention, but there are some caveats. The first is that declaring something a quiz or test doesn't automatically mean it's useful for promoting learning. Tests that rely on recall rather than on recognition have a greater ability to strengthen learning (Rohrer & Pashler, 2010.) The second caveat is that for a quiz or test to be informative to the learner, it must include a mechanism for correction. If a quiz is simply corrected and graded, it is unlikely that much new understanding will occur. Finally, test-taking anxiety does little to enhance recall. Students who are more concerned about grades than about their own learning will view these quizzes with terror. Make sure quizzes are always presented as learning devices and not as tests that merit a grade.

Self-Corrected Spelling

Several of our elementary school colleagues use a process of daily self-corrected spelling to achieve success in conventional or standard spelling (Fearn & Farnan, 2001; Frey, 2010). Each day, students spend a few minutes writing target words as the teacher reads them aloud, and then they correct each word *letter by letter*. They look at each word from left to right, using an editing code for each omission, insertion, or substitution. Students draw a square around the first error in each word, a circle around the second error, and a triangle around the third (students rarely have more than three errors within a single word; if they do, it is a signal that the word is too difficult for them). Students then write the word correctly and turn the paper over to take the spelling quiz again. After they have rewritten the words, they repeat the error analysis and almost always find improvement. This routine should be repeated every day until students spell all the words correctly. The practice effect, and the deliberate focus on errors and correction, improves students' spelling performance substantially. Even though this process focuses on spelling, any number of content area items can be substituted.

Cloze and Maze Procedures

Items that require students to recall information promote retention and learning—a chief intent when checking for understanding. By requiring students to fill in a blank within a reading passage, cloze and maze procedures do just that. The cloze procedure requires the deletion of every fifth, seventh, or ninth word in a selected text passage, with the exception of the first and last sentences, which are left intact (Taylor, 1953). Missing words are not displayed in a word bank, as that would change the task to one of recognition (which is easier) over recall. Here's an example:

Mary had a _____ lamb. Its fleece was white as _____.

The passage itself can be excerpted from a textbook or written by the teacher. A cloze procedure is particularly effective at the beginning of a new unit as a tool to identify preexisting background knowledge students do or do not have. During a unit, a cloze procedure can also serve as a review of the previous day's content. As with self-corrected spelling, the results are not graded but instead used to check for understanding and make instructional decisions.

Younger children, however, may not be able to complete a cloze procedure. Instead, they might be able to perform well using a maze procedure, which includes the first letter of each missing word. In this case, specific words can be deleted to test knowledge.

Mary had a l_____ lamb. Its fleece was white as s_____.

In some cases, maze activities include three choices for each missing word. This requires more recognition than recall, but it may be appropriate for some students:

Mary had a (large, tiny, little) lamb. Its fleece was white as (cotton, snow, daisies).

When using these procedures, be sure to use grammatically and semantically consistent choices for distractors. By eliminating obvious distractors, you can rule out other strategies students may use—such as knowledge of syntax—to choose the correct answers.

Question–Answer Relationships

In addition to finding out about content knowledge, formative assessments can also explore the reasons why students choose correct or incorrect answers. Question–Answer Relationships (QAR) provide students with a decision-making framework for locating information in reading passages (Raphael, 1986). QAR was developed as a means for students to determine whether the relevant information for each question could be found directly in the text (text-explicit) or whether they need to infer the relevant information using a combination of the text and background knowledge (text-implicit). This framework describes four types of questions:

1. *Right There* (text-explicit): Answers to these questions can be located in the text, often in one sentence.

2. *Think and Search* (text-explicit): These answers can also be found in the text, but they may be scattered across several sentences or paragraphs.

3. *Author and You* (text-implicit): The answer is not directly stated in the text and requires the reader to formulate an opinion based on the passage (e.g., "The tone of this passage is . . .").

4. *On My Own* (text-implicit): The student must use his or her background knowledge to answer the question (e.g., "Based on your experiences . . .").

After teaching students about these types of questions and the relationships they have to text, ask students to identify the type of questions they encounter on quizzes and tests that use reading passages. Mr. Luong, for example, includes a second item on each question for his 8th grade science quizzes. "I often give them a short science article related to something we've been studying, and I develop a few questions for them," he says. "I put an additional item next to each question so that they have to choose the type of question and where they found the answer." Mr. Luong says that it gives him further information about the errors students make as they are learning. "Sometimes I have a student who knows the information but looks in the wrong place," he remarks. "Very often they want to take an answer straight out of the text, instead of looking inside their heads. This gives me something to talk with them about and makes learning test-taking strategies much more concrete."

Using Common Assessments to Check for Understanding

When teachers in course-alike groups or grade-level teams meet on a regular basis to examine student work, checking for understanding becomes systemwide. For example, students might participate in a common assessment of their learning at predetermined points (at least every six weeks) in the school year. These are not benchmark assessments but, rather, assessments designed to drive instruction. By contrast, benchmark assessments, such as DIBELS or AIMSWEB tools, are designed to provide a temperature check on how well student performance is aligned with content standards. According to the California Department of Education, benchmark assessments often include performance tasks, but they more frequently use "standardized administration and scoring procedures to help maintain validity, reliability, and fairness" (n.d., para. 1).

This is not to say that benchmark assessments have no value; they do. However, our experience suggests that when groups of teachers create common assessments, scores on benchmark assessments rise faster. Creating an assessment, although it may not be perfect, allows groups of teachers to talk about the standards, how the standards might be assessed, how students are currently performing, and what learning needs to take place for students to demonstrate proficiency. In other words, creating common assessments provides teachers with an opportunity to "begin with the end in mind" (Covey, 2004). In addition, common assessments provide students with test format practice, which has been documented to increase performance (e.g., Langer, 2001). When students understand the genre of the test, they are likely to do better.

Consider the conversation a group of teachers had about an item they had written to check for understanding in their students' ability to use past-tense words correctly. The item, which mirrored the way the skill is assessed on the annual state test, was written as follows:

Choose the correct word to replace the underlined word.

5. The sun <u>rised</u> over the mountains.

    A. raised

    B. rose

    C. rosed

    D. correct as written

Only 22 percent of the students answered this question correctly. Most of them chose *C*, indicating that they had some idea that this was an irregular verb but were not quite sure how to figure out the answer. The ensuing teacher discussion focused on the difficulty of "teaching all of the irregular forms," as one person commented. Another offered, "They just haven't heard these words enough in their language. Their families don't speak English, so they never get to hear these terms at home." One of the teachers in the group said, "I recently heard Stephen Pinker quoted on a podcast saying that 70 percent of the verbs we use are irregular. We have to teach them these; we can't just wait until they listen long enough." This comment shifted the conversation to the various ways that irregular verbs could be taught, and the team agreed to refocus teaching efforts on these verbs, identifying them when they read aloud, contrasting them on the board, and correcting students' usage. They also agreed to reassess students' understanding on the next common formative assessment to see if their efforts had paid off.

Common formative assessments don't need to be multiple-choice tests. At our school, every student responds to the essential questions with an essay and a creative component, such as a video, poster, rap, song, poem, fine art piece, or any of a long list of possibilities. The essay, however, allows us to understand students' thinking about the curriculum and how their writing is developing. The essays are read by a number of different teachers, and each person adds his or her comments to the student's thinking. The following excerpt comes from Brian's essay, written in response to the question "What is race, and does it matter?" Brian is a student with a learning disability who used to write a few sentences for each assignment. His response to this question was 750 words long and included historical photographs.

> Race is a topic that seems to never want to go away. Race is a word that has a strong meaning to it. Race is a four-letter word that should not be tossed around without thinking. Race is not a game; it's part of who you are. But race has been used to hold people back. In education, some people were not allowed to go to school because of their race. That is the focus of this essay. I will talk about race in education from the past to today.

> For a long time it was illegal to teach a slave how to read. People could be put in jail if they helped someone learn to read or write and that person was a slave. They could even be whipped. In the Virginia Law Code of 1819 it said "That all meetings or assemblages of slaves, or free negroes or mulattoes mixing and associating with such slaves at any meeting-house or houses, in the night; or at any SCHOOL OR SCHOOLS for teaching them READING OR WRITING, either in the day or night, under whatsoever pretext, shall be deemed an UNLAWFUL ASSEMBLY . . . [and shall be punished with] corporal punishment on the offender or offenders, at the discretion of any justice of the peace, not exceeding twenty lashes."

> The slave states had laws like this one because they thought it was dangerous for a slave to know how to read and write. They could get ideas and could write to each other. That's why they didn't like Frederick Douglass. He was a black man who could read and write and he was free. He wrote books and made speeches that made lots of people angry. He said slaves should be free. He could read and write and his ideas were read by lots of people. That's one of the reasons people thought it was dangerous for slaves to read and write.

> But education changed when the court case called Brown versus the Board of Education happened. The judge in that case said that "separate is not equal" (americanhistory.si.edu/brown/index.html) and made the schools accept people. That meant that black students could go to schools with white students. When the black students first came to white schools, they had a rough time because no one wanted them. They were trying to change what had already been for a long time. People had so much hatred that they stayed outside the school trying to harass them on their way.

Brian's paper isn't perfect, but it does demonstrate concrete areas of thinking. It also highlights the impact that his social studies teacher has had on him and where he still needs instruction in writing. When teachers read more than 100 of these kinds of responses, there is a strong sense of student achievement and progress—as well as need. Ultimately, that's what common formative assessments are all about—identifying opportunities for feedback and feed-forward.

Looking Back, Looking Forward

In this chapter, we have focused on a number of different ways that teachers can check for understanding while providing instruction. Checking for understanding is not a summative assessment used for grading or accountability but, rather, a formative tool that guides instruction and is part of a formative assessment system that leads into feedback and feed-forward. We have considered the use of oral language, writing, projects and performances, tests, and common formative assessments in checking understanding. Each of these approaches has strengths, and teachers typically use a variety of techniques within each lesson to gauge what students are learning.

In the next chapter, we turn our attention to feedback. We note why feedback, by itself, is ineffective in changing student understanding and achievement and how feedback must be linked with feed-forward instruction. We provide an analysis of the types of feedback, with particular emphasis on corrective feedback. In addition, we focus on the components of feedback necessary to ensure that it contributes to the formative assessment system, including the idea that it should be "timely, specific, understandable to the receiver, and formed to allow for self-adjustment on the student's part" (McTighe & O'Connor, 2005, p. 13).

4

Feedback:
How Am I Doing?

Not too long ago, we hosted some visitors at our school and spent the morning touring classrooms and having conversations. A number of students joined us throughout the tour and provided their insights into what works in teaching and learning. During an especially productive conversation, one of the visitors took out a notebook and pen and asked the student she was talking to if it was all right to record him. She saw the look of surprise on our faces and explained that she was using a smartpen that would allow her to create an audio recording of their discussion while she took notes. Best of all, she could play it back later by touching the pen to the notes and hear exactly what was being spoken at the time she wrote them.

This was all Nancy needed to hear, and within a few days she had a smartpen of her own. The smartpen came with an instruction manual, but she had difficulty setting it up. Fortunately, she turned to Alex, the instructional technology coordinator at the school, who is as patient as he is knowledgeable. He discovered some short videos on the retailer's website explaining how the smartpen worked.

Alex asked Nancy to watch the videos and then asked her to pair her computer with the device. (Alex could have easily done this for her, but he knew that helping her learn how to do it would help her remember how to do it herself in the future.) When Nancy couldn't get the computer to "see" her pen, Alex gave her some indirect corrective feedback.

"This error message is telling you that the Bluetooth isn't activated yet," he said.

Nancy gave him a blank stare, so he reminded her that the manual had the information she needed to solve that problem and move forward. Each time she hit a glitch, she consulted the manual and the videos.

When Nancy succeeded in getting the smartpen to work, Alex said, "I'm so impressed! Not everyone can do this. Just a few months ago this would have been a very difficult thing for you to do, but now look!"

She was excited to show Doug how her new toy worked and demonstrated it for him. Alex then asked her to try out some of the advanced features, such as transferring an audio file from pen to computer and sending it to him. Once again, Nancy was a bit leery but knew that with feedback from Alex she could do it. He provided some instruction and used the manual to show her the steps she should follow. Alex listened to the audio file and told her it came through but was difficult to hear. At this point, she knew how to adjust the volume for recording. Soon enough, Doug bought a smartpen as well and was able to set it up much more quickly because Nancy was able to supply tips based on her errors.

Alex's feedback was critical to Nancy's success in setting up the smartpen. To be sure, instruction was involved, and Alex used resources that had been created by the manufacturer to support Nancy's learning. Alex provided indirect and direct corrective feedback, as well as feedback about Nancy as a learner of technology.

The learning that occurs in classrooms is not dissimilar to this example of making an unfamiliar object work. Students are typically taught something (as Nancy was "taught" by the videos and the smartpen manual) but need more opportunities to make the learning stick. Alex didn't reclaim the learning task, but he gave Nancy useful feedback when she ran into difficulty. The device itself provided its own criterion-based feedback, as Nancy could immediately see whether or not it was working.

In a formative assessment system, students receive feedback about their work and performance and learn about their level of achievement or attainment. It's important to note from the outset, however, that feedback alone is not enough to ensure understanding. Some students are immune to feedback; others become defensive. Ultimately, because feedback shifts responsibility back to the learner, it must be useful to the learner. Inadequate feedback or feedback that is not followed by further instruction (when needed) will discourage rather than encourage learners.

When Feedback Is Just "Feedbad"

As we've noted, not all feedback is helpful. Case in point: A recent graduate came back to visit us. He was enrolled in a college class and had to write several papers for that class. He submitted the first paper in the digital drop box and received the following comments: "On-time. Meets word count requirement. APA style coming along but still has minor errors. Answers question. 8/5/10."

He wanted us to tell him what he could do to get a better grade. We asked to see the rubric for the assignment; there wasn't one. We looked at his paper, pointed out a few APA reference errors, and gave him an electronic resource he could use to check his references next time. We thought the paper read well and was interesting; he had answered the question and made his position known. We were at a loss in our attempt to help him further. The feedback he received was not useful and certainly did not ensure his success on the next task assigned to him.

The act of providing feedback needs to be approached as purposefully as other aspects of instruction. It is important that feedback isn't just evaluative, as with the previous example, but is tailored to the needs of the learner. Feedback can include encouragement as well as correction, and feedback on social and behavioral elements can be as important as academic feedback.

Levels of Feedback

There are four levels of feedback, and these levels influence the feedback's effectiveness. Though each type of feedback is valuable, in specific contexts, the level of feedback must be consistent with the goals that were established as part of the feed-up process.

Feedback About the Task

At this level, the learner receives feedback about how well he or she is performing. When providing feedback about the task, teachers often identify correct and incorrect responses, request additional or different information, and suggest attention to specific knowledge. This level of feedback is often called corrective feedback since it is designed to address, or correct, misunderstandings. Rod Ellis (2009) identifies several types of corrective feedback, including direct corrective feedback wherein the teacher provides the student with the correct information, indirect corrective feedback wherein the teacher identifies an error but does not provide the correction (and may or may not indicate the location of the error), and metalinguistic corrective feedback wherein the teacher provides a clue about the types of errors for the student to correct. Corrective feedback is the most common type of feedback that teachers provide (Airasian, 1997) and is most useful when used to address mistakes. It is much less helpful when students lack information. When students lack information, feedback will not supply that information; they need additional instruction. Examples of corrective feedback include

- "Your solution to number 12 is exactly right."
- "You should reread Section 3 of the text since you've got this question wrong."
- "You'll want to include a transition between these two ideas in your paper."
- "You're pointing to the right one."

Feedback About the Processing of the Task

This level of feedback focuses on the processes a student uses to complete a task or assignment. When teachers understand the processes students need to use, they can provide feedback and scaffold students' use of those processes. As students become increasingly proficient with learning processes, they are likely to transfer that learning to new tasks. To develop students' ownership of processing, teachers use feedback such as the following:

- "Did you use the *first, outside, inside, last* procedure to solve that equation?"
- "It seems like a prediction might help here, right?"
- "I see that you're estimating and that's working for you."
- "When I read this, I wondered if you remembered the descriptive words that you brainstormed."

Feedback About Self-Regulation

The third level of feedback relates to students' self-appraisal and self-management (Paris & Winograd, 1990). Students must learn to assess their ability, knowledge, cognitive strategies, and achievement. In doing so, they must regulate their behavior and actions, working toward the goal that has been established. Here are some examples of this type of feedback:

- "Your contributions to the group really seemed to result in everyone understanding."
- "When you put your head down, you stopped paying attention to the things your group members said."
- "I think you accomplished what you set out to achieve, right?"
- "When you created a graphic organizer, you seemed to get back on track. Did that action help you?"

Feedback About the Self as a Person

The final level of feedback focuses on the student himself or herself. Although this type of feedback may not be effective by itself (e.g., Kluger & DeNisi, 1998), it can be effective when it causes a change in students' effort, interest, engagement, or efficacy. Simply saying "well done" or "nice try" is not likely to result in substantive changes, despite the fact that many students appreciate this type of feedback (Burnett, 2002). In part, this is because generalized feedback does not provide task-specific information. In addition, students use different lenses to evaluate the feedback they receive about themselves. Students who want to be seen as good students receive this type of feedback differently from students who do not want to be seen as successful in school (Klein, 2001). Unfortunately, feedback about the self as a person is often connected with other types of feedback, despite the evidence that it can have a negative effect on learning (Hattie & Marsh, 1995). This is not to say that praise should be eliminated but, rather, that praise should be directed to the effort exerted, and the self-regulation required, for task completion. Examples of this type of feedback, in which praise is attached to the task, include

- "You have great stamina because I see that you've been working on this for several minutes."
- "You're a great student because you're focused on the group dynamics and how the task will be completed."
- "I bet you are proud of yourself because you used the strategy we've been talking about, and it worked for you."

These four levels of feedback are important considerations, but even they are not enough to ensure that feedback is actually helpful. In addition to considering levels of feedback, teachers must consider which comparison group they will use to focus their feedback. As we will see, there are a number of options for comparison groups, and they each have strengths and drawbacks.

Comparison Groups

An important consideration when giving students feedback, and one that is often overlooked, is the selection of the comparison group. As teachers, when we examine student work, we must ask ourselves, "To whom are we comparing this product or performance?" As a case in point, let's consider the following paragraph from Uriel's essay, which he wrote in response to the question "What is race, and does it matter?" During class, his teacher read aloud John Boyne's *The Boy in the Striped Pajamas*, and students selected books from an approved list to help them answer this question. Uriel read Walter Dean Myers's *Monster* and concluded his essay with this paragraph:

What is race, what do you think race means or what it is. How do you think the world would be without race. Would the world be a better place with race or without race. What I always think about is since when did race started to matter and why does it even matter. Race is a word that started to separated us just for our culture, religion, and even the color of our skin. We are all the same, we all live and we start our lifes the same way everybody does so why does a simple word have to matter. If a simple word doesn't affect me and other people so don't let it affect you.

What is your initial reaction to this paragraph? Are you seeing the ideas forming in Uriel's mind? Are you recognizing the argument he's trying to make? Are you identifying some common errors that English language learners make? Are you wondering about his use of punctuation? All of these are appropriate considerations about his submission.

Here, though, are the key questions: What feedback should he be given? How much feedback? On what comparative grounds should his teacher base this feedback?

Criterion-Referenced Comparisons

Most commonly, feedback is based on an established criterion that includes expectations for grade-level work. This is known as "criterion-referenced" because students are expected to meet a specific level of performance. Typically, the criteria involve a cut score, meaning a score at which students are considered proficient. Different assessments have different cut scores. In many school-based assessments, the cut score is 70 percent and would earn the student a *C–* (although some schools use a cut score of 60 percent and pass students with a *D*). When student work is evaluated against the established purpose, the comparison is to the criterion. Feedback, then, is provided based on the expected level of performance. In this case, Uriel would likely receive a failing grade with extensive rewriting and corrections required to have his paper meet the criterion.

Norm-Referenced Comparisons

Even though criterion-referenced comparisons are widely accepted for feedback, there are other ways to evaluate student work. That's not to say we don't want students to reach the established criteria, but, rather, our feedback may need to reference a different comparison group.

A second way to think about feedback, then, is to use a comparison group of other students. In general, this is known as "norm-referenced" because the referent is other students rather than a predetermined, expected level of achievement. Norm-referenced comparisons can provide teachers with information about the relative performance of specific students compared with other students in that same class, school, or district. Thus teachers can determine how individual students respond to the instruction or interventions that are provided.

Many commercially available tests have been norm-referenced, which can also help the teacher identify the ways in which their students perform compared to large numbers of students from across the country. The worry with norm-referenced feedback is that it will be used by students comparatively and competitively, but this happens only if the teacher provides the feedback in that fashion. Feedback of this type should never be delivered by saying, "David did better on this than you did" or "This isn't 3rd grade work."

Instead, when thinking about a peer comparison group, it's useful to consider true peers, not just students enrolled in a specific grade or class. By true peers, we mean students who share similar achievement profiles that may affect their learning. As an English language learner at an early stage of language development, for example, Uriel could be compared with other ELLs at the same stage. If Uriel received feedback using his true peers as the comparison group, the teacher might not focus on the common errors that ELLs make as they move out of early–intermediate stages of language development. Instead, feedback might focus on his ideas and use of punctuation. Uriel writes better than the majority of his true peers who have been assessed at the same level of English proficiency. Accordingly, he might receive a passing grade—let's call it a C+—and the feedback on his paper would likely be less global and extensive than if a criterion-referenced standard were used, but it would certainly be more focused. Instead of responding to a lot of editing marks from the teacher, Uriel might focus on his punctuation, given that the peers in his class did not make these same mistakes.

The challenge of using peers as a comparison group relates to expectations. We do want Uriel to reach high levels of achievement and become a community member who is bilingual. We're not relaxing our expectations, instruction, or interventions. What we are changing is the feedback that Uriel receives about his work.

Individual Student-Based Comparisons

A third comparison "group" is the student himself or herself. Sometimes, teachers are better served to use the student as the comparison so they can monitor growth and development. Again, this is not to say that teachers shouldn't hold high expectations for students and teach them well, but they should focus their feedback based on what the student has already done.

Uriel, for example, made significant progress in the first four months of high school. Formerly gang-affiliated and an active substance abuser, he says that *Monster* was the very first book he ever read "all the way through." His grade point average in middle school was 0.59, and his written response to the question about race was the first time he ever completed an essay. By comparison, the following excerpt comes from the first essay he wrote during the school year. Here is his response to the question "Can you buy your way to happiness?"

> Can yoo by yoor way to Hapiness? In sometimes, money can by happiness but its not in what yoo waste it but in how yoo waste it. The only what yoo can buy hapiness is wisely.

It's clear that Uriel has made a great deal of progress. He has much clearer expression of ideas and better control of the language. Given this, what grade does he get? More important, what feedback might the teacher provide? Using Uriel as the comparison, the feedback on his race paper might read, "You are making very strong points and have clarified your beliefs. You use a number of sources, but let's work on how you cite them. You summarize your thinking well. Can we work some more together on punctuation and transitions?" The important point here is that Uriel needs to be held to high expectations for his achievement and be taught in ways that allow him to reach those levels.

When providing feedback, teachers must determine which comparison group they're using and why. Then—and only then—are they ready to begin the feedback process. If teachers are unclear about their basis of comparison, students will not understand the feedback or be able to use it.

Criteria for the Feedback

Regardless of the comparison group, there are specific criteria to consider when providing students with feedback. We find Grant Wiggins's (1998) criteria—that feedback must be timely, specific, understandable, and actionable—to be especially informative on this subject.

Timely

The evidence is clear—the sooner feedback is given, the better. Feedback is more powerful when it is linked as closely as possible in time with student performance (Bangert-Downs, Kulik, Kulik, & Morgan, 1991). As Susan Brookhart notes, "Feedback needs to come while students are still mindful of the topic, assignment, or performance in question" (2008, p. 10). It's about motivation and relevance. If students are still focused on the purpose or learning goal, they're likely to incorporate the feedback they receive in their future attempts to meet that purpose. If students ask themselves, "When will she ever give that back?" they've probably moved on and are only looking for evaluative comments and a grade, not information that will help them learn the content. If students submit additional, similar assignments without feedback on earlier assignments, there is a missed opportunity for improvement. Even more important, students become frustrated and question the commitment of their teacher to their learning and the importance of the assignments in general.

As a case in point, Nancy still remembers a college class in which she had to submit weekly journals documenting her reflections about student teaching. She enjoyed writing these and looked forward to her teacher's comments. She didn't get comments back on the first week's entries before the second week's entries were due, but she wasn't too worried. She completed the journal entries for the second week and submitted those. When she didn't get anything back in time for review before the third set of journal entries was due, Nancy got a little concerned. She asked herself, "Am I doing this right? Is this important? Should I be spending this much time on this one assignment?" When she finally received feedback during the fourth week of the semester and learned that she had not included all of the components the teacher wanted, Nancy was not happy. She had submitted three more weeks' worth of work that was wrong, and there was nothing she could do about it.

Specific

When students understand what they have done well and what they need to focus on next, they are more likely to make adjustments and improve their performance. When feedback is generic, superficial, or cursory, students are often unable to decide what to do with it and may not even see the relationship between the effort and the outcome. When feedback is specific, students understand what they did well and where they still need to focus.

Grades and points are not feedback. Informing a student that she earned 8 out of 10 points does not tell her what she has done well and what she needs to learn next. Saying "I noticed that you're not always carrying numbers when you add" is much clearer and alerts the student to an action. If the student has been taught to carry while adding, this feedback can change performance and achievement. Of course, if the student has not been taught this skill or doesn't understand it, even specific feedback won't work. In that case, feed-forward is needed. We'll focus on that in the next chapter.

Here's an example of how specific feedback helps learning. When Doug was on a swim team, the coach provided specific feedback about how his hand entered the water. The coach modeled how each hand should enter the water and then demonstrated how Doug's hand was entering the water—not angled or cupped. For the next several workout sessions, the coach watched Doug swim and continued to provide this feedback. At one point, the coach said, "On your third stroke, your hand entered perfectly. Did you feel it? The angle was right there, and it was like the water parted." Yes, Doug felt it and wanted to replicate that exact movement over and over.

Specific feedback isn't limited to coaching situations. In Mr. Bonine's biology class, for example, students complete an individual assignment each week in which they summarize a topic from the week and creatively represent that topic. When Russell submitted his science assignment on cell structure and function, Mr. Bonine gave him this feedback: "I see every structure in the cell clearly labeled in your illustration, but I'm troubled by the membrane that also runs through the middle of the cell. Let's talk and figure out how you might better represent this." Russell immediately knew what he'd done well and where he'd made his mistake. This very specific feedback influenced Russell's future diagramming of cellular structure, including his performance on the final exam.

Understandable

Feedback doesn't do much good if students can't understand it. Just imagine getting feedback from a teacher in a language you don't understand—not much good would come of that. Unfortunately, that's the experience that many students have with feedback. Consider this feedback, provided to a student about his presentation on family systems: "Focus on genograms and less on spiritual ecomaps." Given that these terms were not previously taught and the student didn't know what they meant, at least at the time of the presentation, the feedback did nothing to change the student's learning. Jay McTighe and Ken O'Connor provide a test for this aspect of feedback: "Can learners tell *specifically* from the given feedback what they have done well and what they could do next time to improve?" (2005, p. 12). If not, the student probably isn't going to learn, despite the time that the teacher has put into providing the feedback.

Rubrics are a good way to ensure that feedback is understandable, assuming that students have developed the rubric with the teacher or that the teacher has focused on quality indicators from the rubric in advance of students' initial work on the task. For example, students used Figure 4.1, a rubric on public speaking, to evaluate several professional speakers as well as speeches found on YouTube. Their teacher reviewed and discussed each component of the

Figure 4.1 | **Speech and Presentation Grading Rubric**

	Emerging (0–6 points)	Developing (7–8 points)	Advanced (9–10 points)	Score/ Comments
Organization (10 points)	Ideas are not focused or developed. The introduction is undeveloped. Main points are difficult to identify. Transitions may be needed. There is no conclusion, or it may not be clear the presentation has concluded. The conclusion does not tie back to the introduction. The audience cannot understand the presentation because there is no sequence of information.	The audience has difficulty understanding the presentation because the sequence of information is unclear. Ideas are evident, but they may not be clearly developed or always flow smoothly. The introduction may not be well developed. Transitions may be awkward. Supporting material may lack in development. The conclusion may need additional development.	Ideas are clearly organized, developed, and supported to achieve an intended outcome; the purpose is clear. The introduction gets the attention of the audience, and transitions ensure the audience anticipates content. Main points are clear and organized effectively. The conclusion is satisfying and relates back to the introduction.	
Topic Knowledge (10 points)	The student does not have a grasp of the information and cannot answer questions about the subject. Inaccurate, generalized, or inappropriate supporting material may be used. Overdependence on notes may be observed.	The student has a partial grasp of the information. Supporting material may lack originality. The student is at ease with expected answers to all questions but fails to elaborate. Overdependence on notes may be observed.	The student has a clear grasp of information. Supporting material is original, logical, and relevant. The student demonstrates full knowledge (more than required) by answering all class questions with explanations and elaboration. Speaking outline or note cards are used for reference only.	
Audience Adaptation (10 points)	The presenter is not able to keep the audience engaged. The verbal or nonverbal feedback from the audience might suggest a lack of interest or confusion. Topic selection does not relate to audience needs and interests.	The presenter is able to keep the audience engaged most of the time. When feedback indicates a need for idea clarification, the speaker makes an attempt to clarify or restate ideas. Generally, the speaker demonstrates	The presenter is able to effectively keep the audience engaged. Material is modified or clarified as needed, given audience verbal and nonverbal feedback. Nonverbal behaviors are used to keep the audience engaged.	

Figure 4.1 | **Speech and Presentation Grading Rubric** (*continued*)

	Emerging (0–6 points)	Developing (7–8 points)	Advanced (9–10 points)	Score/ Comments
Audience Adaptation (*continued*)		audience awareness through non-verbal and verbal behaviors. Topic selection and examples are somewhat appropriate for the audience, occasion, or setting.	Delivery style is modified as needed. Topic selection and examples are interesting and relevant for the audience and occasion.	
Language Use (Verbal Effectiveness) (10 points)	Language choices are limited, peppered with slang or jargon, too complex, or too dull. Language is questionable or inappropriate for a particular audience, occasion, or setting. Some biased or unclear language may be used.	Language used is mostly respectful or inoffensive. Language is appropriate, but word choices are not particularly vivid or precise. Some grammar and pronunciation errors are noted.	Language is familiar to the audience, appropriate for the setting, and free of bias; the presenter may "code-switch" (use a different language form) when appropriate. Language choices are vivid and precise, and few errors are present in the speech.	
Delivery (Nonverbal Effectiveness) (10 points)	The delivery detracts from the message; eye contact may be very limited; the presenter may tend to look at the floor, mumble, speak inaudibly, fidget, or read most of the speech; gestures and movements may be jerky or excessive. The delivery may appear inconsistent with the message. Nonfluencies ("ums") are used excessively. Articulation and pronunciation tend to be sloppy. Poise is lost during any distractions. Audience members have difficulty hearing the presentation.	The delivery generally seems effective. However, effective use of volume, eye contact, vocal control, etc. may not be consistent. Vocal tone, facial expressions, clothing, and other nonverbal expressions do not detract significantly from the message. The delivery style, tone of voice, and clothing choices do not seem out of place or disrespectful to the audience or occasion. Some nonfluencies are observed. Most audience members can hear the presentation.	The delivery seems extemporaneous, natural, confident, and message enhancing. Posture, eye contact, smooth gestures, facial expressions, volume, pace, etc. indicate confidence, a commitment to the topic, and a willingness to communicate. The vocal tone, delivery style, and clothing are consistent with the message. Limited use of nonfluencies is observed. All audience members can hear the presentation.	

Source: From Education Northwest. Adapted with permission.

rubric, modeled her thinking about each indicator, and then gave a speech for her students to evaluate. When it came time for them to develop their own speeches, they had a very good understanding of what constituted high-quality work and what was expected of them. When they received feedback on their practice attempts, they understood what they did well and where they could improve.

Actionable

Feedback must provide learners with the opportunity to act on the information provided. Students should be able to self-adjust—review, revise, practice, improve, and retry—based on the feedback they get. In the next part of this chapter, we will discuss forms of feedback that allow for self-adjustment. These criteria overlap with feed-forward, as there are times when students need additional instruction to accomplish self-adjustment.

Andrew's experience is an example of how this might work. Andrew received a social studies quiz back from his teacher with the correct answers provided. The teacher also provided this additional feedback: "You'll want to review the concept of the Divine Rights of Kings and reconsider the lives of Charles the First and Second. Think about the word *restore* and what a monarchy has the power to restore." Andrew wasn't just told his answers were incorrect. He also wasn't just told the correct answers. Instead, he was pointed to some specific information that would help him improve his understanding of the content.

Whether or not feedback is actionable creates different effects on whether and what students learn, as has been shown in studies of testing situations (Bangert-Downs et al., 1991). There was a small (but negative) effect when teachers told students their answers were right or wrong; conversely, there was a moderate (but positive) effect when teachers provided students with the correct answers. Finally, there was a large, positive effect when teachers provided students with explanations about their correct and incorrect responses. This is what Andrew's teacher was doing: providing explanations and resources for students so they could then address their incorrect responses.

Forms of Feedback

Feedback can occur in different ways: (1) teachers can provide oral feedback; (2) teachers can provide written feedback; or (3) students can provide feedback to one another, provided they have been taught to do so. In this section, we will discuss these three forms of feedback.

Oral Feedback

Feedback comes, first and foremost, through spoken channels. As noted previously, it should be well timed and actionable. Beyond that, the setting, structure, and tone of oral feedback should result in positive outcomes for the learner so he or she leaves the interaction with a plan for appropriate next steps.

Put yourself in the place of the student and consider times when you received feedback. As educators, most of us are regularly observed by instructional coaches. What makes these interactions more or less useful to you? You'd probably prefer a setting that is quiet and removed from your peers to a public environment. You'd probably prefer a structure that reflects on what was successful and what was not to one that is evaluative. You'd also probably prefer a tone of voice that leaves you feeling a sense of personal regard and warmth to one that seems abrupt and clipped. These qualitative aspects of oral feedback are just as important to students, regardless of their age, as they are to you. Therefore, consider setting, structure, and tone when providing feedback to students.

Choose an appropriate setting. The choice of setting sets the tone for the discussion that follows. When possible, select a place in the classroom that is physically removed from the larger group. This gives students a place to focus on what is being said and to determine the tone in which it is delivered. In cases where feedback is brief, lower your voice and get closer to the student to foster a conversation. This can assist the student in accurately hearing and processing the feedback.

Structure the response. In order for feedback to be effective, it should be specific and alert the learner to what is correct and what is not. Jeff Zwiers (2008) describes the structure of academic feedback as having three parts:

• A description of the result of their performance. *("Thanks for showing this to me. I can see that you illustrated the life cycle of the frog accurately and labeled each stage in the correct order.")*

• Guidelines concerning what to continue doing or what to change. *("Be sure to check the spelling for each stage. Two of them are spelled incorrectly. Could you check these in your textbook, please?")*

• Encouragement to persist. *("Soon you'll have a terrific graphic of the life cycle of the frog, and it will be easy for anyone to understand. I'm looking forward to seeing what you do next.")*

This structure can take several minutes (or the time that it takes to utter a few sentences), but the results are similar—the learner leaves the interaction knowing where he or she is right now and what needs to be done next. The learner also feels confident that he or she can successfully complete the task.

Use a supportive tone. The message can be lost if the tone is derisive or sarcastic. You'll recall from Chapter 2 that fostering a growth mind-set of intelligence is essential and that reinforcing a fixed mind-set can cause students to give up (Dweck, 2007). Learning is hard work, and a learner's persistence can spell the difference between academic success and failure. In addition to words of encouragement, the qualities that accompany the message, including facial expression, eye contact, and intonation, convey the teacher's confidence in the student's efforts. Distant interactions, rolling eyes, an averted gaze, and a biting tone speak volumes and can discount the message itself, regardless of how effective the words might have been.

Manners also affect the tone of the message. Simple strategies such as saying "please" and "thank you" make the listener more receptive to the message. Additionally, choice empowers students and causes them to take an active role in their learning. We are referring to *real* choices, not the pseudo-choices we have sometimes overheard (e.g., "You can either fix this problem or get a failing grade on this assignment. It's your choice."). Presenting real options can expand each student's vision of what is possible. Consider the following exchange:

Teacher: You've done a terrific job of showing how you solved this math problem. It's clear, and I can follow your logic as you worked your way through the steps.

Student: Thanks. I wasn't sure that I did it the right way.

Teacher: That's a good thought, and the truth is that in math there is often more than one way to do it. I'm interested in how you think, because that makes me a better teacher. Now I've got two suggestions, and I'd like you to decide how to proceed next. One way to answer this word problem would be to draw a picture of what the problem is representing. Another way would be to use math symbols. Both are correct, but I'd like to learn about your mathematical thinking.

Student: So for this next problem, I could show my work either way?

Teacher: Please do so! I'll come back when you signal me, and then you can guide me through your logic.

Although this exchange took only about two minutes, a substantial amount of information was exchanged at both the mathematical and interpersonal levels. In addition, the student leaves the interaction with more confidence in her own thinking, as well as with the comfort of knowing that her teacher will follow up with her.

Consider a formal conference. Many teachers use more formal arrangements to provide feedback to students by conferring with them. These individual conversations are longer (five minutes or more) and intended to focus students on their current work and ability to see their progress from the beginning of the year. Conferring is common in the elementary reading/language arts classroom, but it can happen in any class and in any grade. One reason for its popularity in the primary grades is that it formalizes academic discussion with young children who are not yet proficient at holding such conversations on their own.

Conferring is often focused on multiple assignments rather than a single one. Teachers who take this approach have students keep ongoing work portfolios, or they simply have students keep all their work in a folder or binder. The conference begins with the selection of two or three items (for younger children, this could be done in advance) so that the learner can compare them over time. Irene Fountas and Gay Su Pinnell (2001) describe possible approaches to providing feedback during a reading or writing conference:

- Listen to the student read something aloud (a book or original writing).
- Talk with the student about specific aspects of the student's reading or writing.
- Locate and discuss areas of strength in the student's reading or writing.
- Review the writing notebook or reading log.
- Set new reading and writing goals.

Let's consider the example of Ms. Valentine, who meets regularly with her kindergarten students to confer about their literacy activities and growth. At the beginning of the year, she selects all of the assignments for discussion. As students develop proficiency, they begin selecting their assignments for discussion. She calls Celeste over to a small table with two chairs in the corner of the room, near a sign that says, "Sh! Thinkers at Work." Celeste brings her reading log to show Ms. Valentine.

Ms. Valentine: Wow! Thank you! [reads list] I can see you have already read more titles this month than last. Why is that?
Celeste: I want to beat myself. Like in a race.
Ms. Valentine: I can see that was the goal you gave yourself last month: "I will read 10 books in February."
Celeste: I read 12!
Ms. Valentine: I see that! What was your favorite, and why?

For several minutes, the teacher and student discuss the relative strengths of the titles. When Ms. Valentine asks Celeste to identify her least favorite, Celeste mumbles a bit and then doesn't say much more.

Ms. Valentine: It looks like we hit a bump in the road. Is it hard to remember it?
Celeste: Yeah.

Ms. Valentine: That's the tricky part about reading—the remembering part. Sometimes it can be tempting to just rush through the book so we can add it to the list. What would a new goal sound like?
Celeste: About the remembering. And slowing down.
Ms. Valentine: Let's work on that.

After a minute or two more, they have arrive at a new goal: "To read slowly enough to be able to name what I like and don't like about each book." After writing down her new goal, Ms. Valentine thanks her student for the conversation about books, and Celeste leaves with a new goal based on the feedback she got during the conference.

Written Feedback

Oral feedback offers an immediacy that written feedback cannot. It also offers the chance to accompany feedback with nonverbal behaviors that can strengthen communication. However, teachers can't rely on oral feedback alone because there just isn't enough time. In addition, much of the work students do is written and can't be reviewed until a later time.

As with oral feedback, the tone and structure of written feedback should be respectful and actionable. Most of us can recall receiving a paper that was marked up from beginning to end. Too much of that overwhelms the learner, who might view all those markings as negatives, even if they are not. Some districts have even banned the use of red pens, subscribing to the popular myth that it's the color of the ink that makes a difference. It's not—it's the marks themselves. Conversely, not enough feedback can cause the learners to believe that they didn't make any mistakes when they did or that the teacher did little more than skim the work. A simple way to avoid this is to confine comments to one or more self-adhesive notes. This conveys respect for the work itself (since the teacher doesn't write on the student's paper), and it also gives the student mindful feedback. On long assignments, we use three color-coded notes on the page: one to summarize the paper as a whole, a second for strengths, and a third for next steps. This can also be done on electronic documents, using the software's "track changes" features to write and label comments and to help the learner organize them.

Content of the feedback should reflect one's beliefs about teaching and learning. Quite frankly, it's easier to mark deviations from conventions (e.g., capital letters, punctuation, indenting) than it is to provide feedback about the content. Indeed, this word-and-sentence-level editing occurs far more frequently than content editing. Icy Lee describes 10 ways that written feedback differs from teachers' core beliefs about teaching and learning:

1. Teachers pay most attention to language form, but they believe there's more to good writing than accuracy.

2. Teachers mark errors comprehensively, although selective marking is preferred.

3. Teachers tend to correct and locate errors for students but believe that, through teacher feedback, students should learn to correct and locate their own errors.

4. Teachers use error codes, although they think students have a limited ability to decipher the codes.

5. Teachers award scores/grades to student writing, although they are almost certain that marks/grades draw student attention away from teacher feedback.

6. Teachers respond mainly to weaknesses in student writing, although they know that feedback should cover both strengths and weaknesses.

7. Teachers' written feedback practice allows students little room to take control, although teachers think students should learn to take greater responsibility for learning.

8. Teachers ask students to do one-shot writing, although they think process writing is beneficial.

9. Teachers continue to focus on written errors, although they know that mistakes will recur.

10. Teachers continue to mark student writing in the ways they do, although they think their effort does not pay off. (2009, pp. 15–18)

Seventh grade English teacher Ms. Perez has lots of student papers to read and never enough time to do it. However, she has learned to give meaningful written feedback without overwhelming learners, who might give up instead of persist with further revisions. "I read their whole paper while it's in draft form, but I edit only one 'spotlight' paragraph. I try to choose a section that is representative of the kinds of errors they are making throughout the paper. I turn my attention to that one, and I edit for content first. That's the harder of the two," she says. "The rubric comes in handy for this, because it keeps me focused on the most important elements. On a separate note, I add feedback about the conventions."

A busy classroom can't rely solely on one person's feedback, no matter how thoughtfully it's delivered. Many teachers, therefore, also use peer feedback mechanisms to further support learners.

Peer Feedback

Students who have recently worked or are currently working on similar concepts can provide insightful supports for their fellow learners. These peer-mediated learning experiences foster mutual problem solving and experimentation as students try out potential solutions. Peer feedback commonly takes two forms: peer tutoring and peer response.

Peer tutoring. The effectiveness of peer tutoring has been documented with many students, including those with disabilities (Mastropieri et al., 2001). Technological advances have made peer feedback possible in more settings. For example, some educators have used wireless "bug-in-ear" technology so peer tutors can give immediate feedback to classmates in the middle of oral presentations. The peer tutor can tell a speaker to "slow down" so corrections can be made right away. Researchers have also found that immediate feedback, unlike the delayed feedback that comes after a speech, results in more positive changes, and speakers find it to be helpful (Scheeler, Macluckie, & Albright, 2010).

Student-directed tutoring is also useful when older students work with younger ones to help them learn content. A study of struggling middle school students who tutored elementary learners found that both students gained academically (Jacobson et al., 2001). Whether students tutor same-age peers or students at other grade levels, the relative effectiveness of peer tutoring depends on the accuracy of the feedback offered during the session. In cases where the tutoring partnership is not progressing, feedback from the teacher results in improved quality (Dufrene, Noell, & Gilbertson, 2005). This is an important reminder to educators that a peer tutoring structure can be effective, but it has limitations. Tutors, after all, are not little teachers, and they are likely to miss feedback opportunities that arise when the tutee holds a conceptual misconception; tutors are much more likely to give feedback about factual information, especially when it is directly stated in a text (Chi, Siler, & Jeong, 2004).

High school mathematics teacher Ms. Burow depends on peer tutors to provide additional support and feedback to students who are struggling with content. She looks for particular qualities when identifying potential peer tutors. "I want students who know their math content, of course," she says, "but it's not just that. Just identifying last year's *A*+ students isn't adequate. I'm looking for students who do a good job putting themselves in the role of the learner."

Ms. Burow gets to see these qualities nearly every day in her math classes through the use of productive group work (Frey, Fisher, & Everlove, 2009). Students interact with one another as they consolidate their understanding of mathematical concepts. "I get a good look at their social skills as well as their ability to support the learning of their group members," she says. "It's like tryouts every day. I am looking for kindness but also that quality of giving feedback that is useful and not just focused on the 'right' answer."

Ms. Burow recruits potential peer tutors to work with her in the after-school math tutorial program, and she interviews each one to find out why he or she is interested in participating. "Some of my best math tutors haven't necessarily been the top math kids but are really good at zeroing in on the other person's mathematical thinking," she points out. One student, Sara, is a good example. Ms. Burow calls Sara the Math Whisperer. "She's got this uncanny ability to figure out where the other person is in his or her knowledge and to give good, solid feedback that's going to be useful. Like when Sara was working with Alex, and she said, 'You were doing this correctly up until this step, and then you made a mistake. How could you do this step differently?'"

Sara is an exceptional peer tutor, but Ms. Burow knows that all of her students need her expert guidance. "It's not like all of a sudden I have all these 'mini-mes' in the class and now I can kick back," she says. "They're a great help, but I have to be in those conversations regularly. And not just for the kids who are getting tutoring. I have to monitor the tutors, too. They need feedback just like everyone else. Otherwise, how could they get better?" She trains the math peer tutors in various aspects of learning, especially in giving feedback that doesn't simply provide the answer or that isn't too vague to be of much use.

As Ms. Burows knows, not every student is well suited to peer tutoring. Another approach, which casts a wider net, is the use of peer response in the classroom.

Peer response. Although many classrooms, even ones at the elementary level, rely on peer editing during writing, we find it to be less than satisfactory. First, as with peer tutoring, feedback is limited by the knowledge level of each of the students. If the editor doesn't have a high level of proficiency, or if the writer's knowledge level is low, feedback is likely to miss its mark. In addition, if we, as teachers, are striving to improve our ability to give effective feedback, why should we expect an eight-year-old to be better at it than we are?

However, eight-year-olds (and 18-year-olds, for that matter) *are* good at retelling what they read and understand. Although they need to be taught how to provide effective responses to one another's writing, giving this kind of feedback taps into what they already know how to do. As with peer tutoring, students benefit from being taught how to effectively provide feedback to one another.

Jay Simmons (2003) studied the types of responses given by peers and describes them as belonging to one of several categories. Some are more effective than others, and a few are actually unwelcome:

1. *Global praise.* This is the "good job" kind of praise that doesn't yield helpful information. Simmons refers to this as "cheerleading" and finds that some students use more of this when the teacher is listening as a means to boost their peers' scores.

2. *Personal response.* Comments about the writer's life (or the reader's experiences) can be ineffective at best and intrusive at worst. This feedback shifts the

focus away from the writing and can sound more like therapy than a writing session. Examples include "I went to the zoo last week" (not useful) and "You sound like a very angry person" (inappropriate).

3. *Text playback.* Unlike the previous two categories, this feedback is among the most useful. It involves retelling what has just been read, and it may focus on a specific aspect of the passage. "The introduction got me interested right away" lets the writer know how the reader understood his or her text.

4. *Sentence and word edits.* This type of feedback treads into the teacher's realm, and students are not especially good at doing this. "You used this word too many times" or "This should be a question mark" can leave the writer's paper ineptly and insensitively marked up. In addition, this type of feedback is often incorrect.

5. *Reader's needs.* This is also a helpful kind of peer feedback, as it lets the writer know how his or her text was understood. This can be especially useful for young writers who do not have sequencing under full control. Comments such as "I got confused in this section because there's a new character here whom I don't know" alert the writer to a gap in the information.

6. *Writer's strategies.* These are more difficult to give and not likely to be offered by elementary students and less-adept writers. However, they can be very helpful. This type of peer feedback focuses on the craft of writing, for example: "What would happen if you put this paragraph first so the reader begins with an overview?"

As Simmons notes, "Responders are taught, not born" (2003, p. 684). There are specific ways that students can be taught to use effective techniques while avoiding ineffective and even damaging feedback. Using the techniques outlined in Figure 4.2, 5th grade teacher Ms. Stephenson makes peer response the topic of many focus lessons. Reading her own writing for her students and fielding their responses, Ms. Stephenson shows her students how to incorporate their suggestions into her revisions. When Mariana offers global praise ("It's good, Ms. Stephenson"), Ms. Stephenson thanks her but probes for more specific feedback.

Figure 4.2 | Techniques to Teach Peer Responding

Technique	What the Teacher Does	What Students Do
Sharing your writing	Shares a piece of writing and asks for response. Shares rewrites tied to class response.	Offer comments on the teacher's writing.
Clarifying evaluation vs. response	Shows that evaluation is of product, while response is to writer.	Understand that response is personable and helpful.
Modeling specific praise	Shows how to tell what you like as a reader.	Understand that cheerleading is too general to be helpful.
Modeling understanding	Shows how to tell what you understood the piece to be about.	Understand that reflecting the piece back to the writer is helpful.
Modeling questions	Shows how to ask questions about what you didn't understand.	Understand that questions related to the writer's purpose are helpful.
Modeling suggestions	Shows how to suggest writing techniques.	Understand that a responder leaves the writer knowing what to do next.
Whole-class response	Moderates response by class to one classmate's piece.	Offer response. Hear the response of others. Hear what the writer finds helpful.
Partner response	Pairs up students in class to respond to pieces.	Practice response learned in whole-class session.
Comment review	Reads the comments of peers to writers. Suggests better techniques. Devises focus lessons.	Get teacher feedback on comments.
Response conference	Speaks individually with students, responding appropriately.	Have techniques reinforced.

Source: From "Responders are taught, not born," by J. Simmons, 2003, *Journal of Adolescent and Adult Literacy, 46*(8), pp. 684–693. Copyright 2003 by the International Reading Association, www.reading.org. Reprinted with permission.

Ms. Stephenson: Can you tell me what you like about it, Mariana?

Mariana: I liked learning about when you were our age. I thought it was interesting.

Ms. Stephenson: That's helpful, Mariana, because it gives me some feedback about what is working. Can you tell me what would make it better?

Roberto: I was confused when you said you liked being with friends at the beginning [of the story], but then later you said you liked being alone. Shouldn't it be one or the other?

Ms. Stephenson: That's a good point, Roberto. In my mind it can be both, but it sounds like I didn't explain it very clearly. I'm going to reread that part and see if I don't need a clarifying sentence.

As the discussion proceeds, Ms. Stephenson continues to shape and model her students' responses. In subsequent lessons, she uses students' writing from previous years (with names removed) to provide more experience with analyzing the writing of others. As they become better at peer responses, students begin to volunteer their own writing and practice as partners with their own writing. Ms. Stephenson continues to monitor written comments, providing further feedback about the usefulness of the feedback for the writer. When needed, she meets individually with students who are having difficulty with the process.

"I've been doing this for a couple of years now," explains Ms. Stephenson, "and I think it raises their awareness as writers. I've noticed a real upswing in their writing achievement because they have become more conscious of what works in their own writing. It's like they're learning how to give feedback to themselves as well."

Student Responses to Corrective Feedback

There are a number of ways that students can—and do—respond to the corrective feedback provided by their teachers. Some students take the feedback into consideration and learn something new. This is mostly likely to occur when feedback meets the criteria outlined in this chapter. When these conditions are met, the research evidence on feedback is very positive (e.g., Marzano, Pickering, & Pollock, 2001). When the feedback is timely, specific, understandable, and actionable, students can use it.

Unfortunately, there are only a few studies focused on how students actually use the feedback provided by their teachers (e.g., Treglia, 2008). One of the cautions raised about teacher feedback focuses on the emotional impact of teacher feedback and the potential damage it can do to student–teacher relationships and rapport. Sometimes students read into the feedback that their teacher doesn't like them or that the teacher is rude (Ferris, 1997). In these cases, students are unlikely to use, or learn from, the feedback provided by their teachers.

Assuming that feedback doesn't trigger negative reactions from students and it meets the usefulness criteria, there are specific ways that students typically respond. Dana Ferris (2006) has identified a number of ways:

- *Error corrected.* The mistake was correctly changed based on teacher feedback.
- *Incorrect change.* An identified mistake was changed, but incorrectly.
- *No change.* The student did not make any change.
- *Deleted text.* The text was deleted so that a change was no longer necessary.
- *Substitution, correct.* A change was correctly made by substituting for the identified error.
- *Substitution, incorrect.* A change was made by substituting for the identified error, but an error remains.
- *Teacher-induced error.* Feedback resulted in the student making an error.

Some of these responses are useful; others are not. As we have noted throughout this chapter, feedback is an important part of a formative assessment system, but it may not, in and of itself, result in better learning. For some students, some of the time, feedback works. Other students, at other times, need more instruction that is carefully aligned with the errors they've made or the misconceptions they have.

Looking Back, Looking Forward

In this chapter, we have focused on the ways that teachers can provide students with feedback that improves performance. We have identified four levels of feedback—(1) the task itself, (2) processing the task, (3) self-regulation, and (4) self-referential—and provided examples of each. In addition, we have explored comparison groups and considered the impact on the type of feedback teachers might provide, given different comparison groups. We also noted the criteria necessary for effective feedback, namely, that it be timely, specific, understandable, and actionable. We then turned our attention to the various forms of feedback, including oral, written, and peer.

We acknowledge that, in many cases, feedback is ineffective in changing student understanding. There are a number of reasons for this:

- Some feedback is just plain bad.
- Sometimes feedback isn't timely or specific enough.
- The learner may not understand the feedback.
- The learner may not know what action to take based on the feedback.

This brings us to the focus of the next chapter. Feedback must be combined with feed-forward efforts to increase the likelihood that student learning is facilitated. When teachers make decisions about what to teach based on the performance of their students, learning and achievement improve. In the next chapter, we focus on the strategic decisions that teachers make and the actions they take to link instruction with assessment.

5

Feed-Forward:
Where Am I Going Next?

Hanan joins a small group of 10th grade students at a table with their teacher. They each have a draft of a "Who I Am" poem in hand. Their teacher has provided them with feedback about their drafts and meets with them to provide additional instruction. Other students in the class are working either individually or collaboratively; there are students working on computers and students reading books. There are students talking at a table, producing a poster representing the text they are reading, and students providing one another with peer editing and feedback.

Ms. Anderson, the teacher, begins the conversation when all four of the students in the small group are seated at the table. She starts with an acknowledgment of their efforts, saying, "I enjoyed reading your first drafts. Each of you has taken this assignment to heart and produced a piece that touched me. That's one thing you all have in common from this assignment. The other thing you have in common is the fact that your poems broke the structure. Remember, we talked about the power of the two-line stanza? I'm not saying that you have to use that structure for this assignment, but I thought we could talk a bit further about that structure so that you could think about it as you produce your final copy. Take a look at your papers. Do you see what I'm talking about?"

The students look at the poems they have brought to the meeting. Hanan notices, as if for the first time, that some of her stanzas are two lines long, whereas others are three lines long, and still others are four lines long. She reviews the written feedback from her teacher, focusing on one comment: "Maybe you want to consider revising this using the two-line structure. It might be even more powerful. From what you've read, I was thinking that the two lines might start 'I am _____' and then 'The _____.'"

Ms. Anderson then tells the students, "Maybe it would be helpful to try out the changes while I'm here. Anyone willing to give it a try?" Hanan indicates her willingness to do so. She says, "The first part of my poem has four lines, but now I'm thinking that I'll edit that down to two. I'm thinking that I might use the frame that you wrote in the margin. So, for the first stanza, my poem would read, 'I am a Curious George/The first and the last, the beginning and the end.'"

Ms. Anderson invites other students in the group to comment on the revision.

> **Edgar:** That's a strong way to say that. I get it even more. You're saying that you are curious, totally. And maybe even that it gets you into trouble. The old way you said it, I didn't get that.
>
> **Deon:** I think your second part is good. You make it a bigger point when you say "first and last" and "beginning and end." Before, I didn't get what you meant in the last line. Now it sounds like a prayer.
>
> **Hanan:** Thanks. That's what I was trying to do. I think that this works better. I get it. Let me try the next part.

The conversation continues, and Ms. Anderson invites students to take into account the feedback she has provided. When students struggle with understanding, Ms. Anderson is available to feed instruction forward using questions, prompts, and cues. She does not tell students what to do but, instead, guides their understanding through interaction, allowing students to make revisions as they see fit. Hanan's final poem can be found in Figure 5.1.

Hanan's progress in writing in an unfamiliar genre (poetry) illustrates the fits and starts that mark real learning. Rarely is it a linear process of relentlessly

---

Figure 5.1 | Hanan's Revised "Who I Am" Poem

I am a Curious George
The first and the last, the beginning and the end.

I am one who understands the misunderstood
The unheard and the unraveled.

I am one who hides so much and shows very little
The one with strange hellos and great goodbyes.

I am creative and unique
The one who wonders why people are so judgmental.

I am who I am because of each of you in my life
The one who benefits from all of the love, and no love.

I am who I am for what I have said and did not say
The one who has heard and did not hear.

I am who I am because of all of I have done
The one who has seen and experienced.

I am Hanan
The one who matters, even when I don't matter to you.

---

forward movement, where new knowledge is neatly layered on existing knowledge. As much as we might wish for a strictly behavioral theory of learning, where exposure to information would lead directly to results, we know too much about learning and cognition to cling to such a naive view. Nevertheless, there remain teaching practices that mimic such a belief, especially in endless lectures that rarely rise above simple dictation.

Learning, which depends on knowledge and skill acquisition, is complicated. For example, we know that knowledge can be described across several dimensions. There is declarative knowledge, driven mostly by facts, and procedural knowledge, which is the application of those facts in a sequential way to achieve something. Then there is conditional knowledge, which involves judgment about how and when to do something (Anderson, 1983). Each represents a higher degree of knowledge integration, and each represents an area of potential misconception or error.

A sport such as tennis is a wonderful example of the different types of knowledge. To correctly name the equipment (e.g., racket, strings) and label the basic movements (e.g., forehand, backhand, volley) is declarative knowledge, and it forms the basis of knowledge about tennis. At the procedural level, the budding player must know the rules of the game, how to keep score, and how to swing accurately at the ball. At the conditional level, though, the player makes more strategic choices. He or she must not only hit the ball accurately but also put a topspin on the ball to make it difficult to return or hit the ball to the back of the court when the opponent is positioned close to the net. In short, it's the degree of conditional knowledge that sets apart Serena Williams and Rafael Nadal from the rest of us. Each attempt to integrate different types of knowledge represents another potential opportunity for misconceptions and errors.

Misconceptions

Students bring forward their misconceptions from previous instruction and experiences. These misconceptions are further influenced by students' developmental levels, their perceptions of school and learning, and even their expectations for what will be true. Misconceptions are known to be persistent and somewhat intractable unless they are addressed directly. In fact, it is not unknown for learners to selectively excerpt facets of new knowledge to support and strengthen existing misconceptions. Here are some examples of common misconceptions:

- American Indians lived in teepees because they couldn't afford houses.
- Seasonal changes occur due to the earth's distance from the sun.
- Multiplication of fractions will result in a larger number.

Simply directing students to read a text is not an ideal means for correcting misconceptions. In a comparative study of college freshmen, students who held misconceptions had poorer recall of scientific text and made more errors than those who did not have misconceptions (Kendeou & van den Broek, 2005). Interestingly, both groups used the same number of reading comprehension behaviors, such as interrogating the text, making inferences, and summarizing. In other words, the reading process itself went just fine; students simply got different things out of it.

This reminds us that "conceptual change is socially mediated" (Allen, 2010, p. 156); that is, the shift from misconception to accurate conceptualization is much more likely to occur in the presence of others. New understanding is needed to replace misconceptions, which are stubbornly resistant to change. Discussion, conjecture, evidence of claims, and questions are all necessary steps to change one's thinking about deeply held misconceptions.

Returning to the example that began this chapter, when Ms. Anderson met with Hanan, she recognized that Hanan had some misconceptions about poetry. Ms. Anderson had anticipated and addressed some common misconceptions in her initial teaching, such as the ideas that all poetry must rhyme or that it is written only in stanza form. However, she thought that students would be able to identify the use of pattern in the example poem, but Hanan did not apply this to her own poem. When Ms. Anderson met again with Hanan, they discussed this point explicitly, and the teacher provided additional instruction so Hanan could grow beyond her basic understanding of the form.

An analysis of misconceptions and errors is essential in a feed-forward system since it allows the teacher to make purposeful decisions about which students need further instruction and in what areas. In addition, error analysis provides the teacher with the basis for precise teaching and reteaching of concepts that students do not yet fully understand.

Error Analysis

Analyzing the errors that students make is very informative for teachers who want to implement a formative assessment system. Errors are interesting because they represent the current understanding of the student. Errors can be used to plan instruction, especially instruction that is tailored to current student needs (Kramarski & Zoldan, 2008). It is important to remember that the errors students make are perfectly logical to them; they don't know that they're making errors. When this is the case, simply pointing out the error may not be effective in changing student achievement.

In contrast to simple error identification, error analysis allows us to devote half our grading time to feed-forward and half our time to feedback. In contrast, earlier in our careers, we devoted all of our grading time to feedback. Of course, this approach didn't work, and students often tossed all of our hard work in the trash. This is a really important point. Providing feed-forward cannot result in consuming more time. We're not looking for something that takes teachers away from their students and families. Therefore, we recommend that teachers devote half of their grading time to feed-forward analyses, as we think it's a better use of time.

Miscues

One of the most common error analysis systems involves analyzing the errors that readers make while reading. There have been studies of miscues for deaf students (Girgin, 2006), English language learners (Wurr, Theurer, & Kim, 2008), and struggling readers (Moore & Brantingham, 2003). There have also been studies examining the ways in which parents attend to the miscues of their children (Mansell, Evans, & Hamilton-Hulak, 2005).

The general idea of a miscue analysis is to note the types of errors a reader makes while reading. Kenneth Goodman (1967) identified three sources of errors that readers often make. For example, while reading the sentence "Then we spotted the bug," the reader might make errors with regard to

- Letters within the word (graphophonic cues), such as saying *bed* for *bug*.
- Semantic content of the word's context, such as saying *spider* instead of *bug*.
- Syntax of the sentence in which the word is found, such as saying *girl* for *bug*.

Though all three of these miscues represent mistakes, the subsequent instruction differs based on the type of error that is made. There are formal coding systems for miscues (e.g., Goodman & Burke, 1972), as well as systems for collecting running records (Clay, 2010) that are beyond the scope of this book. For our purpose here, it's important to note that the errors students make guide our instruction.

Error Coding

Thankfully, there is a simpler version of error coding that allows teachers to identify errors and determine which students made each type of error. As teachers evaluate student work, they identify the errors that students make and catalog them.

For example, Mr. LeClair analyzes "What Sustains Us?" draft essays, specifically looking for students' use of mechanics. He wants to identify students in need so that he can plan instruction based on those needs. He doesn't need a laundry list of the mistakes students made, especially errors that he isn't going to address on this draft. He previously gave students feedback and feed-forward information about their ideas and thesis development. As is represented in Figure 5.2, specific students make specific types of errors—errors we can teach them how to correct. Before delving into the errors that Mr. LeClair identifies, it's important to note that students also received feedback on their papers. For example, Jessie, a student who made a number of errors, received the following written feedback:

> Your ideas are clear, and you have a lot to say. Your transitions between paragraphs motivated me to read further. You maintained the present tense throughout the paper, which was great to see. I'd like for you to run the spell-check program on this paper and see which errors you can find. We will meet to talk further about some additional mechanics.

Jessie doesn't need a comprehensive list of things she did wrong. That won't help her perform any better on the next assignment. If her teacher had compiled a comprehensive list of her errors, Jessie might have been compliant and

Figure 5.2	**Error Analysis**				

Date: ___10/12___   Topic: _"What Sustains Us?" draft essay; focus on mechanics_

Error	Period 1	Period 2	Period 3	Period 4	Period 5
Mid-sentence capitalization	JC			AA	
Colons and semicolons	JC, JT, AG, DL, TV	EC, MV, WK		AA, SK, MG, EM, BA, TS	HH, DP, MR, CH
Ending punctuation	JC, AG, SL	WK, MW		AA, BA	MR
Subject–verb	JC, JT, DL, MM, SL, ST, ND	RT, VE, VD, CC		AA, MG, SC, PM, LG	DP, DE
Tense consistency	DS	SJ, JM		AA, TR, PC	DE
Spelling	JC, MM	WK, RT, AG, SJ		AA, MG, BA, GL, PT, DO, DE, LR	SR, DC, MF

changed them all, but whose paper would it have become—her teacher's or hers? What Mr. LeClair recommends—the spell-check function—is something that she can do and should remember to do in the future. This bit of feedback is timely, specific, understandable, and actionable.

During the feed-forward sessions, Jessie receives additional instruction on specific areas of need. For example, Mr. LeClair hypothesizes that errors related to colons and semicolons are an overgeneralization error and that Jessie (and the others) did not fully understand the lesson about this less frequently used type of punctuation. Mr. LeClair gives the group of students who made this error additional instruction designed to address their mistake.

The error analysis allows Mr. LeClair to group students according to need, which is one of the evidence-based recommendations for formative assessment systems. We have to provide students with the correct information and a rationale for that correct information. That's the easy part. Providing it to students who need it, and not everyone else, is the hard part. Using this type of error-analysis tool guides teachers to provide "just-right" instruction based on their students' needs.

Ms. Nguyen, a math teacher, uses a very similar tool to analyze student work samples. She has several error types already identified on the tool, such as calculation error, wrong formula, and incorrect problem setup. She also leaves several blank lines to identify the errors that are less common or are unique to specific problems that her students solve. In this way, she anticipates errors, has a coding system to record the errors, and has a plan to address those errors. Similarly, Ms. Murray, who teaches science, uses the error-analysis tool to review the exams she gives. Rather than use exams solely for summative purposes (such as grades), Ms. Murray analyzes the mistakes her students make and determines what they still need to learn from her. On one of her tests, nearly every student misses a question about messenger RNA. When she finishes coding, she realizes that she had recorded almost every student's name for that specific error. She concludes that she didn't teach this concept very well and that she needs to reteach it to every one of her classes.

As these examples demonstrate, error analysis is useful for identifying who needs reteaching so the teacher can make decisions about grouping. Although Ms. Murray discovers that reteaching is necessary for the whole group, Mr. LeClair sees that he needs targeted small-group instruction in each period to reach those students who still are not successful. It would be a waste of academic time for him to teach the entire class about mid-sentence capitalization; it would be negligent to ignore the needs of a small group of students. These small groups, though, are likely to need more that just a scaled-down version of his initial lesson. Instead, they need guided instruction to scaffold their understanding.

Guided Instruction

The term *guided instruction* has existed for decades and describes the shift from direct explanation and modeling to a state where learners assume some of the cognitive responsibility under the tutelage of a teacher. There are several purposes for using guided instruction (Fisher & Frey, 2010):

- To check for understanding and to determine what students have learned and where they continue to struggle.
- To reveal partial understanding and other misconceptions that might lie just below the surface.
- To use scaffolds in the form of prompts and cues as needed to strengthen a learner's knowledge.
- To provide direct instruction and modeling when the learner is not successful despite scaffolding.
- To foster productive success in which students see themselves as capable and their efforts rewarded.

We have seen a number of "guided instruction" lessons over the years that were actually small-group focus lessons (i.e., the teacher models and demonstrates, discussed further in Chapter 6) without the release of cognitive responsibility. Legitimate reasons exist for modeling, demonstrating, and providing direct explanation, such as building background knowledge or making up missed instructional time due to student absences. However, these techniques should not be confused with the instructional moves a teacher purposefully makes when providing guided instruction.

Ms. Hernandez, for example, uses guided instruction with her 2nd grade students during social studies. After modeling how she makes sense of a passage from the textbook on how to use a map, she meets with small groups of students for further guided instruction. Charmaine, Tim, Derek, and Thien-Nhut—their social studies texts tucked under their arms—meet Ms. Hernandez at a table with a hand-drawn map of their neighborhood.

"Let's take a look at the map, and I want you to notice the grid pattern that's on it," she begins. "It's got letters going up, and numbers starting here," she says, pointing to the map. "We're going to look at this map of our neighborhood and figure out what coordinates to use." She explains the purpose further, telling them that they will use resources, including the textbook and one another, to plot locations on the map using small paper flags inserted into a base of modeling clay.

Lined up on the table are several flags labeled with the names of a local grocery store, their elementary school, the local park, the public swimming pool, and other landmarks. Ms. Hernandez begins by asking questions about how coordinates are used on maps so that she can ascertain how much her students retained from her focus lesson on map coordinates. When Tim answers incorrectly, she first asks him to think about his recent experiences with using a grid in mathematics. Tim still isn't able to make the connection between his background knowledge and this new task, so Ms. Hernandez shifts his attention to a source.

> **Ms. Hernandez:** Take a look on page 37 in your book. That's the page we just read together. [The students open their books and find the page.] Remember how I found the location of the police station on the map at the bottom of the page?
>
> **Tim:** Here it is, right here. [pointing to the police station in the book]
>
> **Charmaine:** But she wants us to say where it is using . . . what they's called?
>
> **Ms. Hernandez:** We read about them in the book.
>
> **Charmaine:** [looking in the book] Here it is! *Coordinates.*
>
> **Ms. Hernandez:** Everyone put their finger on that word: *Coordinate.*

Ms. Hernandez continues to question Tim and other members of the group as they place the flags on the map and label each with the appropriate map coordinates. During the next 10 minutes, Ms. Hernandez gathers information about the extent to which each learner understands the focus lesson, clarifies her students' understanding using prompts and cues, and provides additional modeling and direct explanation when the prompts and cues are insufficient. During this guided instruction, students use academic language (e.g., coordinates) in their discussion, furthering their understanding of the concepts Ms. Hernandez is teaching.

In 1997, Kathleen Hogan and Michael Pressley reviewed and summarized the professional literature and identified eight essential elements of scaffolded instruction. Notice how many of these elements were discussed in previous chapters:

- *Engage the student and the curriculum before instruction begins.* The teacher considers curriculum goals and the students' needs to select appropriate tasks.
- *Establish a shared goal.* Students might become more motivated and invested in the learning process when the teacher works with each student to plan instructional goals.
- *Actively diagnose student needs and understanding.* The teacher must be knowledgeable about content and sensitive to the students (e.g., aware of their background knowledge and misconceptions) to determine if they are making progress.
- *Provide tailored assistance.* This may include cueing or prompting, questioning, modeling, telling, or discussing. The teacher uses these strategies as needed and adjusts them to meet the students' needs.
- *Maintain pursuit of the goal.* The teacher can ask questions and request clarification as well as offer praise and encouragement to help students remain focused on their goals.
- *Give feedback.* To help students learn to monitor their own progress, the teacher can summarize current progress and explicitly note behaviors that contribute to each student's success.
- *Control for frustration and risk.* The teacher can create an environment in which the students feel free to take academic risks by encouraging them to try alternatives.
- *Assist internalization, independence, and generalization to other contexts.* The teacher helps students be less dependent on his or her extrinsic signals to begin or complete a task and also provides the opportunity to practice the task in a variety of contexts (Larkin, 2002).

The teacher's use of scaffolds is purposeful and follows a model that allows for this release of responsibility. Figure 5.3 is a flowchart of the decision-making process that teachers use during guided instruction. This should not

Figure 5.3 | **Guided Instruction Flowchart**

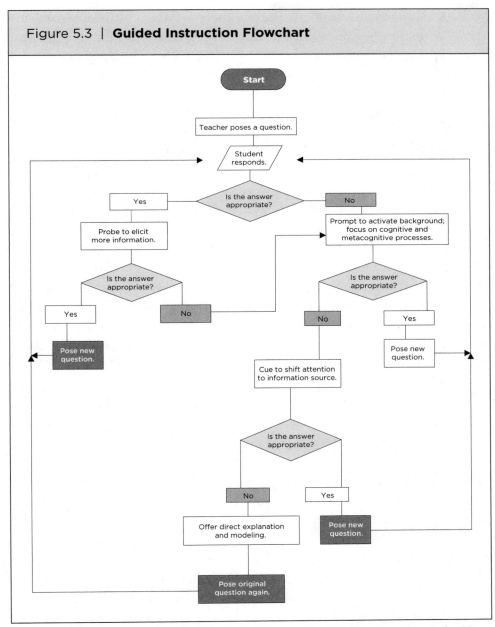

Source: From "Identifying instructional moves during guided learning," by D. Fisher and N. Frey, 2010, *The Reading Teacher, 64*(2). Copyright 2010 by the International Reading Association, www.reading.org. Reprinted with permission.

be misinterpreted as a template because there is quite a bit of improvisation that goes on during such lessons. Instead, it should be a map for how cognitive responsibility is transferred from teacher to learner. In the next section, we will provide examples of these instructional processes in more detail.

Scaffolds in Guided Instruction

The use of scaffolds is a hallmark of guided instruction. The notion that the guidance of a knowledgeable adult can increase the learning capabilities of a student can be traced back to the work of psychologist Lev Vygotsky, whose theory of the zone of proximal development has informed educational practice for decades. Vygotsky described this zone as the theoretical space between what a learner can do alone and what he or she can do with guidance from an adult. David Wood, Jerome Bruner, and Gail Ross (1976) were among the first to describe this guidance as scaffolding. They based much of their early work on extended observations of interactions between mothers and very young children. The researchers were struck by the mothers' capacity to shape their children's learning without taking over the task completely. The relative success or failure of each child's attempts at a task (such as stacking blocks) would inform the mother about what to do next. If the child was not successful, the mother would provide more overt assistance; if the child completed the task, the mother would introduce a new task. In every case, the child received encouragement as well as scaffolded instruction.

We have witnessed this behavior hundreds of times outside the classroom. Recall, for example, the time when you learned how to drive a car. You were taught how to correctly identify the necessary components to drive a car (e.g., key, mirror, accelerator, brake) while an adult instructor sat in the passenger seat. You were reminded to put on your seat belt, adjust the mirror, and turn the key. At times, the instructor asked questions to make sure you understood the directions and asked you to describe what you would do next. As you put the car in reverse to back out of the driveway, the instructor again coached you to check the rearview and side mirrors for pedestrians and cars. Getting behind the wheel was an important phase in your learning, as this is where you began consolidating the knowledge needed to perform a complex act.

Reading Recovery teachers have a great term for this. (Reading Recovery is an instructional intervention for struggling 1st graders.) They describe their practice as seeing how students apply skills and concepts "on the run." Emergent readers are busy coordinating graphophonic, syntactic, and semantic cueing systems to accurately translate the squiggly lines on the page into letters and sounds and then translate those letters and sounds into words and sentences. Similarly, emergent math learners must coordinate what they know about numeracy, counting, and number patterns as they learn how to add. Whether you teach reading, math, or driving, your learners need many opportunities to practice what they are learning in environments that will shape their attempts safely.

These are the scaffolds that are most evident in guided instruction:

- Asking *robust questions* to check for understanding.
- Providing *cognitive and metacognitive prompts* to activate background, procedural, reflective, and heuristic knowledge.
- Providing *cues* to shift the learner's attention to a source.
- Providing *direct explanation and modeling* to reteach when the learner is not able to successfully complete the task (Fisher & Frey, 2010).

Taken together, these elements of scaffolding make guided instruction a necessary component for formative assessment because it bridges what is known with what will be learned. In addition, the active participation of learners is viewed as a necessary step in meeting instructional goals.

Robust Questions to Check for Understanding

Guided instruction begins with questioning to check for understanding. As discussed in Chapter 4, checking for understanding addresses the question "How am I doing?" The teacher must determine what the student knows and doesn't know at a given moment in time. This determination is at the core of formative assessment, and it is the starting point for guided instruction.

We call these questions robust questions to emphasize the intention behind the scaffold. At times, questions can sound more like quizzing, or what Doug calls "Guess what's in the teacher's brain?" Indeed, the practice of questioning has a somewhat checkered reputation. Courtney Cazden (1988) and others have identified the most common classroom discourse practice as Initiate-Respond-Evaluate (IRE). This teacher-directed approach appears to be soliciting the "right" answer, as opposed to exploring why the student thinks a certain way.

Teacher: What's the chemical symbol for gold? (*Initiate*)
Student: Au. (*Respond*)
Teacher: Good. (*Evaluate*) What's the symbol for mercury? (*Initiate*)

Admittedly, we've chosen a pretty limited question to illustrate IRE. After all, there is only one correct answer for the teacher's question. There is certainly a place for this type of question in discussion, but as an isolated question, there's not much room to build. Furthermore, in this example, the teacher has closed off any possibility of further discussion because he or she immediately moves on to ask about mercury. Let's look at this example again using a different teacher response.

Teacher: What's the chemical symbol for gold?
Student: Au.
Teacher: Good. Let's talk more about that. We know it's a precious metal, but why? What's one characteristic that would make it so precious to people?
Student: Well, it's pretty.
Teacher: That's true, but lots of metals could fit that description, like iron and copper. You're getting close to a characteristic, but it's not quite there. You're talking about jewelry, right?
Student: Yeah, like the gold jewelry I've got on right now.
Teacher: So stay with that. Iron can be pretty, but you don't see much iron jewelry. What is it about gold that makes it so good for jewelry?
Student: Well, you can shape it.
Teacher: There you go! The word we use for that is *malleable*. It's soft enough to shape but strong enough to keep its shape after it's been formed. Now let's keep going. What's another characteristic of gold that makes it precious?

This teacher isn't questioning to quiz; he or she wants to check for misconceptions and partial understanding. In this case, the student has some limited information about gold but only a vague sense of what makes gold different from other elements on the periodic table. The teacher uses a more robust method of questioning in order to ascertain what the student knows and doesn't know and then uses that information to figure out what to do and say next.

There are many types of questions, and researchers have organized them into different categories, including *productive* and *reproductive*. Productive questions invite students to synthesize and evaluate information and create new ideas, whereas reproductive questions require students to recognize and recall. Although both are important, there should be a balance between the two. In a study of classroom teachers' questioning habits, researchers found that 76 percent of the questions asked were reproductive in nature. A further analysis of the data reveals that the ability to ask different types of questions is related to experience—novice teachers (defined as having fewer than four years of experience) ask reproductive questions 85 percent of the time, but experienced teachers (with more than four years of experience) ask the same type of questions only 68 percent of the time (Tienken, Goldberg, & DiRocco, 2009).

The biggest problem with asking so many reproductive questions is that it limits scaffolding to recall and recognition. Ask an interesting question, and you can provide more interesting scaffolds. Let's return to the student–teacher exchange about gold. What if one or more of these questions were asked instead?

- "What is it about gold that makes it so precious to people?"
- "Why don't people make jewelry from mercury?"
- "Gold's atomic structure allows it to combine with some elements but not others. What characteristics would another element have to possess to make it possible to combine with gold?"

Any of these questions would provide the teacher with a richer picture of what a student knows and doesn't know, and the responses would help the teacher give feedback about what needs to be taught next. Questions themselves are not "good" or "bad." Rather, when a teacher's questioning range is limited, his or her ability to instruct is also limited. Therefore, knowing various types of questions is a good first step in improving instructional practice.

Types of Questions in Guided Instruction

Questions can be asked for a variety of purposes, but in guided instruction, they are an entry point for further scaffolding. We have organized questions into six categories that describe the most common and frequently used types. Our focus here is on the intention of the question, especially with regard to what the teacher hopes to uncover.

Elicitation questions draw on previously taught information, including background knowledge and prior experiences. For example, when 1st grade teacher Ms. Columbus asks, "Tell me what you already know about zebras," she invites learners to access the knowledge they acquired during their field trip to the zoo the week before. Based on the accuracy and depth of students' responses, she can pose more robust questions to determine what her students know and do not know.

Elaboration questions follow an initial question and are intended to get learners to expand on an idea. The length of students' responses is a good indicator of language development, especially at the preschool and elementary levels (Rice et al., 2010). After Edgar answers the elicitation question with the response "They're black and white," Ms. Columbus follows up with an elaboration question: "Could you tell me more about that?"

Clarification questions also ask students to provide further information. Unlike elaboration, though, clarification questions focus on the ambiguity of an answer. Gabriella, another student in Edgar's group, chimes in and says, "They're all in lines." Ms. Columbus then asks her, "I'm not sure what 'all in lines' means. Can you draw the lines for me so I can see what you mean?" This question challenges Gabriella to clarify what she meant.

Divergent questions require learners to draw from more than one source of information to synthesize their understanding. After the group discusses the zebra's stripes, Ms. Columbus wants to ascertain their ability to use information about zebras with previously taught knowledge about their main predator—the lion—which is color blind. She remarks, "I've heard that zebras have stripes to hide themselves from lions, but it seems like black-and-white stripes would get you noticed! So what do you know about lions that makes these stripes a good disguise?"

Heuristic questions require students to use informal problem-solving skills. Ms. Columbus uses this type of question when she shows students a black-and-white photograph of a herd of zebras standing together on the savannah, a view similar to what a lion would see. "There are lots of zebras here, but it's hard to tell where one ends and another begins. How could you count these?" Gabriella indicates that she would count the heads and tails, and Edgar says he would identify the outline of each animal. Another student in the group offers that if you count all the heads and tails, you might end up with too many zebras. In each case, these students use heuristics to solve a problem.

Reflective questions invite opinions and speculation. As Ms. Columbus's guided instruction draws to a close, she says, "Mr. Montoya's class is going to the zoo next week. What information about zebras should his students know before they get there?" Although there is no single correct answer to this question, the question is asked in order to observe students' ability to think metacognitively.

It is useful to prepare questions in advance of a lesson so you can ask for an array of information. We like to create a question bank of at least one of each question type so we remember to use some of them during the lesson. Robust questions are used to check for understanding, and student responses provide a preliminary formative assessment into what they know and do not know. When students exhibit misconceptions or partial understanding, prompts should take center stage.

Prompts for Cognition and Metacognition

When it comes to guided instruction, it's all about intention. Robust questions are used to *assess*, whereas prompts get the student to *do* something cognitively or metacognitively. Prompts can be offered in the form of a statement or a question, and they move students from response to action. Prompts can be further classified into two categories: cognitive and metacognitive. Cognitive prompts elicit information, and metacognitive prompts bring the act of learning to the forefront. Cognitive prompts typically ask students to apply background or procedural knowledge to a situation, and metacognitive prompts ask students to think reflectively.

Prompts are important because they help learners identify which information is meaningful for resolving a problem. As previously discussed, novices are not particularly adept at figuring out what is important and what isn't, but experts know exactly what information they need. Novice learners do not gather information as efficiently to resolve a problem. Prompts are intended to help them gather and apply relevant information.

Background Knowledge Prompts

These prompts draw on students' previous learning. We've all witnessed this occur hundreds of times in our classrooms: A student is reminded of something from a previous lesson, only to gasp and exclaim, "Oh, yeah!" Background knowledge prompts remind students to use what they already know in order to respond. Consider the following student–teacher exchange concerning the Gettysburg Address:

> **Teacher:** That short speech is considered one of the greatest speeches of all time, and it got printed in the newspapers of the day. What's a major theme of that speech? (*elicitation*)
> **Student:** That everyone had to stick together, like being in a family when it's fighting.
> **Teacher:** Say some more about that. (*elaboration*)
> **Student:** Like there was a war and everything.
> **Teacher:** True, but I'm also thinking about some other events that were taking place in 1863. Think about a violent uprising we were discussing yesterday. (*background knowledge prompt*)
> **Student:** [pauses, then brightens] Oh, yeah, the riots in New York—what were they called? The Draft Riots. 'Cause people didn't want to have to go be soldiers, and the rich people were buying their way out.

Teacher: You're right, and the Draft Riots happened just days after the Battle of Gettysburg. So think about the speech again and consider what you know about the riots. Why would Lincoln want to make a point about sticking together? (*background knowledge prompt*)

Process and Procedure Prompts

Students learn a variety of processes and procedures designed to sequentially describe the steps for completing a task. Examples include the FOIL method to multiply binomials or the steps involved in the writing process. When Mr. Bonine's biology students dissect a sea star, he uses procedural prompts to help them complete the task.

> **Mr. Bonine:** Think about what you do first. (*procedural prompt*)
> **Brandi:** We have to get it so we can see the underbelly.
> **Mr. Bonine:** Right, so you're positioning the specimen. That's the first step. What's next? (*procedural prompt*)
> **Stanley:** Now we pin it so it won't move when we open it.

Mr. Bonine uses procedural prompts to get students started on a complex task; although they knew the steps declaratively, this is the first time they are putting them into action. Both background knowledge and procedural prompts are intended to move students to a cognitive action, but at other times we need students to notice their own learning. Metacognitive, or reflective, prompts cause students to pay attention to their own thinking as a means for taking action.

Reflective Prompts

At times, students must use what they know to reflect on their learning. Metacognitive learning activities are intended to foster this self-awareness. Such activities include writing about the accomplishment of one's goals, keeping an interactive journal, or debriefing a lesson. Third grade teacher Mr. Wasserman, for example, meets with several students each day just before dismissal to reinforce the day's learning. He often uses reflective prompts to encourage more active participation in learning. During one such conversation with Emelie, he realizes that she doesn't have a strong grasp of the content presented during the lesson on American Indian trickster tales. Mr. Wasserman spends several minutes asking questions to check for understanding with cognitive prompts, and Emelie's understanding becomes more complete. As a reflective prompt, he asks, "What do you know now that you didn't know before?" Emelie is able to tell him that these stories are different from the *pourquoi* stories they had read earlier in the week and that now she knows to look for a moral in each story rather than figure out how the story explains the origin of something.

Heuristic Prompts

Physical education instructor Ms. Clarke uses heuristic prompts frequently in her educational practice to improve her students' techniques. During a soccer unit, she asks 7th grade student Marta to notice the way she approaches the ball when kicking it from the left.

> **Ms. Clarke:** I noticed that you're trying to kick the ball with the toe of your shoe. Do you remember why that doesn't work? (*elicitation*)
> **Martha:** Because it's too pointy. It sends the ball in a different direction.
> **Ms. Clarke:** Yep. But it seems like it's hard for you to remember that when it's time to kick it. I used to draw a star on the part of my shoe where I wanted to make contact. What could you do to help yourself remember? (*heuristic prompt*)
> **Martha:** [pauses to think] I could tell myself, "Kick with the inside of my foot!" just before I do it?

Using cognitive and metacognitive prompts encourages students to apply information strategically to arrive at new conclusions. However, prompts are not always enough, and further scaffolds may be necessary. The next level of scaffolding is called cueing. Cues shift students' attention more deliberately to the sources of knowledge they need.

Cues to Shift Attention

The purpose of a cue is to shift the learner's attention to a source of information. This differs from a prompt in that it is more overt and typically offers a direction for learners to follow. Cues do not give students the answer; rather, they provide learners with a path to follow in order to arrive at the answer.

The notion of shifting attention is important here, and it makes us think of the "color commentator" on a sports broadcast. During the 2010 Winter Olympics, Nancy was excited to watch snowboarder Shaun White compete. The snowboarding event was not familiar to Nancy, nor was much of the terminology associated with the sport. Most important, she didn't know what to watch for. It just seemed like a lot of people whizzing around in the snow and through the air. The crowd reactions helped a bit, but the cheers and groans often came too late to help her figure out what had just happened. The color commentator, though, was able to slow down the action and direct Nancy's attention to the things that mattered. When he explained the difficulty of the moves and slowed down the video replay so she could see the number of rotations, Nancy's admiration for the sport and athletes grew. When White executed a Double McTwist 1260, the commentator drew lines on the screen with a Telestrator and helped her notice the two flips and three and a half spins. The expert pointed out the most important features to the novice.

In similar fashion, a teacher points out the most important features of a learning activity to his or her students, perhaps highlighting a passage in a text or pointing to the portion of a math problem where the error lies. Like robust questions, cues are a scaffold offered during guided instruction. Cues take back some (but not all) of the cognitive responsibility from the learner. Various cues are used in classrooms, and many are paired together, such as when a verbal cue accompanies a gesture.

Visual Cues

These use color, light, or graphics to highlight something important. Examples of visual cues are all over the textbooks students use. There are words in bold, which are sometimes printed in a separate color that further categorizes them. Students use highlighters to select text, or they place a sticky note on a page to take notes or bookmark an important point. Many visual cues are text-based, but other visual cues use pictures, color, or symbols. For example, restroom doors are marked with signage in graphic form. Traffic lights use color to signal when to stop and when to go. The spines of schoolbooks feature symbols that let you know at a glance what grade level the book is intended for.

Consider the following examples of visual cues. When Tori gets stuck on a worksheet's directions, her teacher underlines the key words so Tori will be able to follow the correct sequence of steps. Dan has difficulty finding information in the book he is reading, so he and his English teacher compose notes together on a sticky note and then affix them to the appropriate pages. Because Jennifer keeps getting lost at her new high school, the guidance counselor circles on her schedule all the classes she has that are in the East building.

Verbal Cues

These cues can stand alone or be paired with other cues. Verbal cues are not about words per se but, rather, about the rate, intonation, expression, and emphasis that accompany the words. At times, a verbal cue may simply repeat what a student says in order to draw his or her attention to the statement. These cues are not given in a sarcastic manner; instead, they are given to help the listener focus on the message. When Tori has trouble with the worksheet directions, for example, her teacher says, "First you'll do *this* part," and simultaneously underlines the section title. After writing a sticky note about the introduction of a story's antagonist, the English teacher slowly hands the note to Dan and says, "You're going to put this note . . . ," drawing out the words as she says them. As the guidance counselor circles room numbers on Jennifer's schedule, he tells her, "All of *these* are in the East building. All the others are in the West building."

Gestures

Perhaps the most common cues used in classrooms are gestures. They are so ubiquitous that they are seldom discussed. Yet evidence shows that well-timed and meaningful gestures promote concept development in subjects as diverse as mathematics (Arzarello, Paola, Robutti, & Sabena, 2009) and science (Ping & Goldin-Meadow, 2008). The effective use of gestures that match the spoken language is considered a marker of second-language learning.

Gestures may include those that illustrate a concept, such as raising both hands upward while discussing a volcanic eruption or pinching the index finger and thumb close together while reading the word *tiny*. Other gestural cues are for location, such as pointing to a sentence on the board, and still others are used for motion, as when a music teacher holds his or her hand up to tell the orchestra to stop.

Physical Cues

Younger children may not accurately interpret some gestures, especially those that are more conceptual. In these cases, teachers might rely on physical cues that direct attention more overtly. Examples include tapping a student on the back of the hand while reading to regulate the pace or providing hand-over-hand assistance for a child learning cursive writing. Because of the physical contact, these strategies are less commonly used with older students, who are more adept at responding to other types of cues.

Environmental Cues

A final type of cue can be found in the classroom environment. Walls are typically filled with information to be used as resources, not merely decoration. Language charts, word walls, manipulatives—all of these are examples of environmental cues. The secret to using these cues effectively is to position them in proximity to the people who use them. It is typical for a kindergarten teacher to transfer a big book the class reads during shared reading to an easel near the writing table where students compose a response to the story. A student struggling to spell the word *principle* is likely to correct his or her error after the teacher points to the "Commonly Misspelled List" posted in the classroom. This is an example of a gesture paired with an environmental cue.

A skilled teacher uses prompts and cues as scaffolds to get students to do cognitive work. Keep in mind, though, a major purpose of guided instruction: It is a formative assessment to determine which parts of the lesson "stuck" and which might need to be reviewed or retaught. With this in mind, expect that direct explanation and modeling will occasionally need to occur.

Direct Explanation and Modeling to Clear Up Confusions

There's a simple comfort in believing that students merely need to be taught something once and then we can move on to the next topic. This belief is delusional, of course. Guided instruction exposes what students know and what they don't know, and we can use prompts and cues to scaffold partial understanding. However, despite good teaching and committed students, learning doesn't always happen the first time around. That's when the teacher must temporarily reassume cognitive responsibility to provide students with direct explanation.

Direct explanation should not be confused with direct instruction. By contrast, the emphasis of direct explanation is on identifying and modeling the technique(s) to be used, thinking aloud about the internal decisions that you make, and monitoring application of the technique(s) while the learner tries it again (Alfassi, 2004). In the case of guided instruction, the technique has likely been taught at least once already, but it hasn't yet been learned at a level that students can successfully execute it. If you've learned how to play a musical instrument, for example, you realize how important each step is. An effective piano teacher isn't going to say, "No, like this!" and play the song again. She's going to identify what she'll do next ("I'm going to play this passage for you. Watch how I shape my hands like they're paws"). As she demonstrates the correct hand position, she thinks aloud so that the learner can recognize if he or she is doing it correctly ("I'm keeping the backs of my hands slightly arched. I know if I keep the knuckles slightly bent, it will give me the finger flexibility I need"). After demonstrating the relevant technique, she'll turn it back to the learner and monitor his or her ability to duplicate that technique ("Now you try it, and remember to keep your hands in the paw position. I'll watch your hands while you read the music").

So it is with direct explanation in the classroom. Take the case of Ms. Chung, a 2nd grade teacher working with a small group of students who are completing a science lab on capillary action in plants. Several days ago, they placed white carnations in water that had been colored with bright blue food coloring. They kept an observation sheet and noted the changes they saw over the next two days. Now the flowers are bright blue, and the leaves have darkened from their original green color. Because their teacher had established the purpose before they began, the students understand that the purpose of the lesson is to witness capillary action in a plant. Nevertheless, the sight of the formerly white flowers—now blue—overwhelms them. Despite their observations, they are not able to arrive at the conclusion that the colored water was transported up the stem and into the leaves and flowers through the vessels. Prompting about capillary action does not work; neither do cues back to their science textbooks. Therefore, Ms. Chung brings a paper towel to this group of students.

"I'm going to show another item that uses capillary action, just like the plant did. This will happen faster than with the plant, so I am going to tell you what I am observing, too," she explains. "I want you to watch what I'm watching and decide what it is that makes the capillary action happen."

She pours a small puddle of blue water on the table and then lowers a corner of a paper towel onto the top of the water. "See how I am barely touching the water? Let's watch to see what happens." Immediately, the blue water travels up the paper towel. "I'm getting really close so I can see it. Get close so you can see it," she says. "Wow! I can see little lines in the paper towel, and they're turning blue. They're getting longer! I know those little lines are the fibers in the paper towel. The fibers are pulling the blue water up into the towel." Ms. Chung then immerses the corner of the paper towel into the water. "I know that's capillary action at work," she says. "Those little fibers are making the capillary action happen. Without them, I know this wouldn't work because there wouldn't be a path for the water to follow."

Finally, she returns cognitive responsibility back to her students. "I want you to look closely at the stems of these carnations. Look for something that reminds you of these fibers. You can break the stem to get a better look. Use the magnifying glass from your science kit if you need to." The students are now enthusiastic about close observation. "I see little thready things," exclaims Kevin. "Me, too! And they're blue!" says Johanna. "That's what does the pulling. Those thready things, like in the paper towel," offers Alexander. Within a few moments, the students in this group have a clearer understanding of capillary action and how it occurs in plants.

"Now think about capillary action and the roots of the plant. Does it happen there, too?" asks Ms. Chung. And so the cycle of asking robust questions begins again.

Looking Back, Looking Forward

In this chapter, we provided an overview of feed-forward as a component of a formative assessment system. We started the chapter with a discussion of misconceptions and error analysis. These mistakes and errors represent what students know; what they don't know; what they use but confuse; and what they think, based on the teaching they have experienced thus far. Remember, the mistakes that students make are perfectly logical to them. Teachers use their knowledge of these mistakes to determine what to teach next (and how to teach it). When mistakes are identified, feed-forward instruction can begin.

As part of the feed-forward instruction, teachers check for understanding using robust questions. A range of questions can be useful in uncovering misconceptions and errors. In addition, teachers use prompts to facilitate students' cognitive work. Prompts can be cognitive or metacognitive in nature, but they do not simply provide students with missing information. When prompts do not work to resolve errors, teachers can use cues. Cues shift the learners' attention to a specific source. This is not done to provide students with the answer either but, rather, to help students notice information that was missed. If both prompts and cues fail to resolve the error, teachers rely on direct explanations that ensure students experience some level of success. This process of guided instruction prevents students from developing learned helplessness, a state in which they become dependent on the teacher for answers.

In the next chapter, we consider the ways in which formative assessment fits with an instructional framework. We focus on the implementation of the gradual release of responsibility framework and how this framework provides teachers with choices for addressing student needs. We also discuss ways that instruction can be differentiated and the role of the leader in creating and implementing a formative assessment system.

6

Building a Formative Assessment System

We have argued that a formative assessment system requires attention to feed-up, feedback, and feed-forward. Together with a thorough checking-for-understanding process, these components guide teachers' actions so student work is used to inform the learner and the ensuing instruction that the learner receives.

This system of formative assessment works best when it is nested within an instructional framework that allows for differentiation and response to student needs (Fisher & Frey, 2007b). In the absence of such a framework, teachers struggle to find the time to address students' needs. Just think about teachers who use lecturing as the primary structure for imparting information. These teachers talk for the majority of the instructional time, and even when they set a purpose, check for understanding, and provide students with feedback, there really isn't any way to feed-forward other than deliver the lecture to the whole class again. This structure prevents teachers from implementing a formative assessment system because it is unlikely that the entire class needs to hear the information again. Invariably, some students will disengage and might even get in trouble, academically and behaviorally.

Here's a case in point. We observed a 4th grade teacher who structured her class in two primary ways. Either she talked to her students, or they worked independently while she provided individual help. This teacher had a purpose for every lesson and gave students feedback on their worksheets and other independent tasks. She also used student work to provide and inform individual tutoring. Nevertheless, even she realized this approach wasn't working. As she said, "I spend so much time grading work, and then I try to get to every kid who needs it. I never seem to have enough time to grade or to tutor. There has to be a better way."

Thankfully, there *is* a better way. When teachers implement an instructional framework, they use assessment information to make instructional decisions. This is what formative assessment is all about—taking action based on student performance. It's not just providing individual help but also intentionally ensuring that students' needs are met in ways that build their confidence and competence.

With a few tweaks to her teaching, this teacher saw student achievement improve and her own satisfaction increase. She didn't need to radically change everything about her classroom; instead, she needed to let student performance guide her whole-class, small-group, and individual lessons. She still had to meet standards and expectations, and she still gathered assessment information about students' current performance. The adoption of an instructional framework simply provided her with a way to channel the data into action. The instructional framework that we describe below provides teachers with a structure that includes small-group instruction, productive group work, and modeling.

Gradual Release of Responsibility Instructional Framework

The gradual release of responsibility model of instruction suggests that cognitive work should shift slowly and intentionally from teacher modeling, to joint responsibility between teachers and students, to independent practice and application by the learner (Pearson & Gallagher, 1983). This model provides a structure for teachers to move from assuming "all the responsibility for performing a task . . . to a situation in which the students assume all of the responsibility" (Duke & Pearson, 2004, p. 211).

The model is built on several theories:

- Jean Piaget's work on cognitive structures and schema (1952).
- Lev Vygotsky's work on zones of proximal development (1962, 1978).
- Albert Bandura's work on attention, retention, reproduction, and motivation (1965).
- David Wood, Jerome Bruner, and Gail Ross's work on scaffolded instruction (1976).

Taken together, these theories suggest that learning occurs through interactions with others, and when these interactions are intentional, specific learning occurs.

Our own implementation of the gradual release of responsibility has four components (Fisher & Frey, 2008a):

1. Focus Lessons. Here, the teacher establishes the purpose of the lesson and models his or her thinking. The purpose should be based on the expected learning outcomes, such as standards, and be clearly communicated to students. Teacher modeling should provide students with examples of the thinking and language required to be successful.

2. Guided Instruction. In guided instruction, the teacher strategically uses questions, prompts, and cues to facilitate student understanding. This can be done with whole groups of students but is probably more effective with small groups that are convened based on instructional needs. During guided instruction, the teacher focuses on releasing responsibility to students while providing instructional scaffolds to ensure that students are successful.

3. Productive Group Work. Students work in collaborative groups to produce something related to the topic at hand. To be productive, the group work must involve students using academic language and being individually accountable for their contribution to the effort. This phase of instruction should provide students with an opportunity to consolidate their understanding before they apply it independently.

4. Independent Learning. Finally, students apply what they have learned in class and outside of class. Many independent learning tasks are used as formative assessments, designed to check for understanding and to identify needs for reteaching. Of course, independent learning tasks should not come too soon in the instructional cycle, since students need practice before they can sufficiently apply knowledge in new situations.

Though we present the components in this order, they can be used in any order, as long as every lesson contains all four of them. For example, a science colleague of ours starts with an independent writing task (a journal entry) designed to activate students' background knowledge. She then asks each student to discuss his or her response with a partner (productive group work) and add notes from this discussion to the journal. She then establishes the lesson's purpose and models her thinking while she reads from the science text (focus lesson). With this added information, she asks partners to join with another pair to form groups of four. Together, students create collaborative posters that synthesize and summarize their understanding of the question (productive group work). Students write in differently colored markers on the poster for individual accountability and talk about what they are writing. As they do so, the teacher moves around the room and checks for understanding (guided instruction). Students know that she will stop and ask them about what they've written, so they refrain from writing something that they don't understand. When she stops by one of the groups, she notices that the group included incorrect information on the poster. She asks about this information and then gives the group a prompt to encourage critical thinking about the comment (guided instruction). When this does not result in understanding, she cues the students to reread a specific paragraph of the text, at which time they understand the mistake and correct it.

Differentiation Within the Instructional Framework

As we have noted, differentiation is an important aspect of the teaching and learning process. It's critical to motivation. Teaching from the gradual release of responsibility instructional framework provides teachers with an authentic way to differentiate their instruction.

Interestingly, not all aspects of the curriculum need to be differentiated. Yes, we can differentiate along the lines of content, process, and product (Tomlinson,

2001). We can be even more selective about how we differentiate, using formative assessment information, when we consider an instructional framework. To get a better sense of how differentiated instruction works within our instructional framework, let's look inside a 6th grade classroom as the class explores ancient China—specifically a unit on the Silk Road.

The teacher, Ms. Coville, establishes the purpose of the lesson, which is to identify the challenges faced by people who used the Silk Road. Students have already learned why the Silk Road was developed. Anticipating misconceptions, Ms. Coville focuses on the fact that the road itself was not made of silk; rather, it was used to transport many things, including silk. As part of her modeling, Ms. Coville displays pictures and illustrations of the geography of the Silk Road, including the deserts, mountains, rivers, plains, and rocky land that travelers had to traverse. As she thinks aloud, Ms. Coville describes her thinking about the dangers of the road. For example, while displaying an image of a snowy mountain, she says, "I see the amount of snow, and I'm thinking about the lack of shelter. I'm wondering where the travelers stayed and how they kept warm. I'm also wondering what they had to eat. I guess that they could carry some food with them, but it would probably run out if they had to stay in these mountains very long. I don't see any source of food here, so I'm thinking that this added to the danger of the trip."

There really is no need to differentiate either the lesson's purpose or the teacher's modeling. Given that the purpose should be aligned with standards, it would be inappropriate to lower the expectation for certain students. While modeling, the teacher provides students with examples of grade-level thinking and vocabulary, which all students need if they are to be successful. As part of the modeling process, the teacher anticipates and handles any tricky parts and makes his or her thinking explicit, thus making differentiation unnecessary.

Following Ms. Coville's modeling, students move into productive group work. On this particular day, they read about the dangers along the Silk Road in reciprocal teaching groups (Palincsar & Brown, 1984). As they read, they take turns using the comprehension strategies of summarizing, predicting, questioning, and clarifying. Their individual accountability includes their notes from each of the conversations and the summary that each student writes after completing the reading. Listening in on one of the groups reveals their use of academic language and thinking.

> **Taryn:** I'll start because there are several ideas to clarify. So, the first word that got me stuck was *cavalry*. I looked this up on Google, and it means soldiers who fought on horseback. So, it's like their version of the army, but they had horses. That makes sense because they didn't have other forms of transportation back then.
>
> **Michael:** And for a summary, I'm thinking that the main idea here is that the road was dangerous because of the conditions. Like it says, the terrain changed a lot. What I thought was interesting was that merchants didn't go all of the way to the end of the road. They paid other people to take their goods.
>
> **Andrea:** And that makes me have another question. Why would they pay people to carry their goods and other stuff?
>
> **Tyler:** Because it was too dangerous. And some people were better at certain parts of the road. So, like people who learned how to survive the desert would get paid to get the goods through that part, and then they'd give them to the next person who had to take the silk through the mountains, for example.
>
> **Andrea:** And how far did the goods go?
>
> **Michael:** All the way to the end of the Silk Road. They went from China to the Mediterranean Sea.
>
> **Tyler:** And my prediction is that we'll learn more about what happened to the goods when they moved from person to person through different parts of the Silk Road. I predict that there will be some goods that never made it and that they cost a lot because of the conditions.
>
> **Taryn:** I agree. I think that each person will charge for their part.

There are several ways that teachers can differentiate the productive group work tasks their students complete. Remember that productive group work is designed to give students an opportunity to consolidate their understanding and use academic language. It also provides data that teachers can use to plan instruction.

One of the ways to differentiate productive group work is through the use of peers. Peer support is a powerful way to ensure that students learn (e.g., Fuchs, Fuchs, & Burish, 2000). This is not to say that we should simply turn our classrooms over to students and let them have at it, but there should be opportunities for students to collaborate on tasks. Peers can provide language support, give prompts and cues, and motivate one another to complete tasks. Peers are an effective way to differentiate the teaching and learning process.

There are a number of other ways to differentiate instruction during productive group work. In the Silk Road example cited earlier, the teacher can provide different groups with different texts. Differentiating the content in this way ensures that students read and discuss texts at their respective levels of proficiency. The teacher can also assign specific comprehension strategies to each group rather than to individual students within each group. Groups of students then work toward a common goal (instead of several distinct goals fracturing each group), and time spent on task is increased. The teacher can also differentiate the product that students are expected to create during the group work portion of the lesson. In this case, one student might be provided with sentence frames to support summary writing, and another student might be provided with a word bank to use while taking notes.

While her students work in productive groups, Ms. Coville meets with small groups of students for guided instruction. As we described in the previous chapter, guided instruction involves the strategic use of questions, prompts, and cues. It's de facto differentiation, since the questions, prompts, and cues teachers use are based on what they know about their students and how those students respond to instruction. For example, when Ms. Coville meets with one group of students, she realizes that they do not understand the concept of the trade route, namely, that China also received goods from other countries. She then prompts and cues students to build their understanding of the use of the Silk Road as more than simply bringing silk to cities near the Mediterranean Sea. She focuses on the text, which includes a discussion about India and Rome.

Ms. Coville: Remember we talked about the idea of trade earlier this year.
Wilson: Yeah, it's when people exchange things. They make a trade.
Nixon: Like this [holds his pencil] for that. [points to a notebook]
Wilson: You get something in return.
Ms. Coville: And the Silk Road is a trade route.

Audrey: So they traded. Like silk for money.

Ms. Coville: Only money? Did China need anything?

Graham: They had a lot. They traded food, flowers, and a lot of other stuff. It says right here. [points to a paragraph of the text]

Ms. Coville: Think about products from India.

Audrey: They had a lot of cotton.

Graham: So did China want the cotton? 'Cuz cotton grows on a plant, and maybe China didn't have that. They had the worms for the silk.

Wilson: They could trade it. I'll give you silk, and you give me cotton.

Audrey: That makes sense, because people want what they don't already have.

Nixon: That's probably why they took the risk of going on the Silk Road, to get stuff that they wanted and trade with the stuff they had.

Although guided instruction is, by its nature, differentiated, the same cannot be said of much of the independent learning that is assigned to students. Independent learning tasks—both in-class work and homework—also need to be differentiated. The goal of an independent learning assignment is to ensure that the task is challenging but not frustrating. When students are asked to apply what they have learned, they deserve support in doing so.

Differentiating independent work can be as simple as taking a basic assignment and changing one of its requirements. For example:

- *Number of items.* Some students might be asked to complete only four problems, but other students might complete six.
- *Type of items.* Some students might respond to questions, whereas others write questions, and still others summarize information.
- *Input routes.* The teacher can provide different reading materials or sources of information, such as websites.
- *Output routes.* Some students might digitally record their responses, whereas others write theirs, and still others are interviewed in front of the class.

Even though independent work is differentiated, students should still be held accountable for content related to the established purpose. We are not suggesting that some students be held accountable for less information or a reduced understanding, but students must be allowed to demonstrate understanding in different ways. Here's what's important: A formative assessment system should include a differentiated curriculum and instruction. Differentiation provides teachers with an opportunity to assess student learning and then create instruction that is targeted to students' needs instead of instruction on material that students already understand.

The Instructional Framework in a Formative Assessment System

The gradual release of responsibility instructional framework is flexible and provides teachers with different mechanisms to support students. We've already discussed differentiation as a support system. Now we turn our attention to the way that this framework can be used to integrate formative assessment data. To do this, we'll look inside three different classrooms. In each case, the data from the formative assessment system suggest a specific action.

Often, as we've already discussed, teachers use guided instruction to address the errors and misconceptions they uncover while looking at student work. In effect, teachers lay the groundwork for "what's next" on each student's path toward mastery. To do this effectively in small groups, the other parts of the instructional model (i.e., focus lessons, productive group work, appropriate independent learning) must be in place. Students must have something meaningful to do while the teacher guides the learning of others—and that "something" is not simply additional worksheets.

Guided instruction, though, is not the only answer to the question "What next?" In some cases, students need additional consolidation opportunities, such as those that are provided during productive group work; in other cases, they need additional teacher modeling; and sometimes student performance data suggest that students are ready for additional independent work and summative assessments.

Consolidation Opportunities

Students in Ms. Arraza's geometry class have been learning about the properties of triangles so they can use those properties in their proofs. Ms. Arraza has already established purpose and modeled her thinking about triangles and how to use their properties (such as exterior angles and remote interior angles) to solve problems. Students have engaged in a number of productive group tasks, and Ms. Arraza has guided several groups when they encountered errors and misconceptions. On their exit slips, most students did not correctly identify the properties of an equilateral triangle and how those properties could be used to figure out related angles.

Ms. Arraza takes this information into account as she plans the next class session. She believes that she modeled this concept well and hypothesizes that her students need additional consolidation opportunities to really be able to use the information. Her feed-forward plan is integrated into the instructional framework in the form of additional productive group tasks. She decides to give each group a different prompt that requires using the properties of an equilateral triangle in a proof. In their groups, students solve the proof on a large piece of poster paper, and each group member contributes information in a differently colored marker. In this way, Ms. Arraza can assess each student's contribution and then use it as a basis for her questions, prompts, and cues.

The first round is difficult, and several groups make errors. Ms. Arraza selects two groups who use the information from the prompts correctly to share their thinking with the whole class. She then asks groups to trade prompts and try the process again. As before, each member of the group writes in a differently colored marker. As they do so, they talk about the information provided in the prompt and what they know about triangles, especially equilateral triangles. Most groups refer to the two preceding presentations and recount the process those groups used to solve the proof. As the groups work, Ms. Arraza talks with students about their work, questioning, prompting, and cueing to guide their understanding. She identifies two additional groups to share because they demonstrated success on the second problem.

She then asks students to trade prompts again. Like before, the groups get to work. Students talk with one another and write their responses using the colored marker assigned to them. Ms. Arraza continues with her guided instruction, scaffolding student understanding. During this third round, all but one of the groups correctly solve the proof. Two groups present their work to the rest of the class, and Ms. Arraza says to the group, "This practice seems to be helping you solidify your knowledge. Let's do one more just to be sure."

Again, the groups trade prompts and get to work. Ms. Arraza observes the group with the incorrect answer to determine where their mistakes are occurring. This group does not make a mistake on this proof. In fact, all of the groups get the proof correct. Ms. Arraza's hypothesis is correct. Her students needed additional time with their peers to apply what they learned and to talk with one another about the content. At the end of the period, the students complete an individual exit slip with a new problem that requires them to use the information they learned during the class period. Ms. Arraza is pleased with the results and knows that her class is ready to move forward.

Modeling

Mr. Perry's 5th graders are working hard on their persuasive essays. They've already brainstormed and written their first drafts. They've talked with peers and received peer feedback. They've edited their drafts and are now ready to turn them in. Mr. Perry is excited because the topics his students have chosen are interesting and current. He can't wait to dive into these papers and see what his students think. When he does, however, he's disappointed. In paper after paper, his students fail to persuade. The papers are good and successfully inform. They're just not persuasive.

Mr. Perry thinks long and hard about his students' work. He decides they need more modeling beyond the idea generation, word choice, transitions, peer responses, and editing already done every day. Of course, he could work with each student individually, but he'd never get to all of them before time ran out. He could also have them work in productive groups, but they would need to know what to pay attention to. Modeling is where the data tell him to go. He realizes that without additional modeling, his students will not understand the difference between informing and persuading.

The next day, Mr. Perry models the difference between telling someone about something and getting a person to do or believe something. This is what he says:

> I know that there are different purposes for writing. Sometimes I want to write
> to tell someone about something. Like when I wanted to tell Principal Jenkins

that the class had done very well on the math exam. That was information that I thought she would like to have. Other times, I want to convince someone of something. I know that I have to be persuasive because that person might not agree. There is a difference in how I write to convince someone. I'm thinking that our class should go to the museum to collect data. I have to convince Ms. Jenkins that this is a good use of the field trip money. I'll start writing some ideas that might convince her. I have a list of words that I can use when I want to persuade someone.

Mr. Perry decides to have his students try their hand at writing a persuasive letter to the principal after he starts the letter so they will practice the content together. Periodically, he stops them and models his thinking about being persuasive as opposed to being informative. By the end of the day, his students have edited drafts of their persuasive letters. Mr. Perry wants to read through these letters to determine if his students are ready to tackle the revision process or if they need additional modeling.

Summative Assessment and Independence

Ms. Swain's 2nd graders are familiar with the life cycle. They have read a number of different books about plant and animal life cycles, and their teacher has modeled her thinking about life cycles. They have germinated seeds and documented the life cycle. They have worked in groups to analyze the life cycle of insects. Over the course of several weeks, these students gained a deep understanding of the concept of a life cycle. The student performance data Ms. Swain collected over the unit provide a clear message—these students are ready for any summative assessment that might be thrown at them.

Ms. Swain uses a science fair as one of the summative assessments. Each student randomly draws a life cycle topic and creates an information display about that topic. In past years, Ms. Swain worried about her students and wondered if they were ready. This year, though, she's not worried at all because she used a formative assessment system in which student work feeds forward into an instructional model that fosters greater understanding. When Jack draws a card with the topic "Illustrate the Mosquito's Life Cycle," Ms. Swain reflects on the various learning opportunities that have prepared Jack for this task. She remembers, for example, one occasion when Jack was working with a group to illustrate another life cycle and comments that this was good preparation for him. Ms. Swain also remembers when Jack got confused and thought that eggs came after pupae and how her prompting and cueing, and his subsequent reading, clarified the correct sequence for him. Yes, Jack and the rest of the students are ready for their summative task. It is time for them to assume responsibility and independently demonstrate their understanding of the content.

Questions and Answers About the Formative Assessment System

There are some common questions that people ask about establishing a formative assessment system. The following sections constitute our responses to several of the most common questions.

Can you buy a formative assessment system? Yes. We regularly use the assessments that come with our adopted textbook. These commercially available materials help us design assessments and leveling questions. They are a good resource and starting point for creating a system specifically tailored for our students. What you can't buy is the teaching that goes with the formative assessments. That's where teacher expertise and experience come into play. Internalizing a system of using student performance data is the goal of the formative assessment system, and that goal requires a teacher who fully understands how students learn.

Can a formative assessment system include teacher-made instruments? Yes! There is a lot of power in the act of creating assessments oneself. Every time we've developed an assessment, we've gained clarity about the standards and expectations that students need to meet as well as the instructional routines we will use to ensure that students are successful. Of course, creating one's own assessments means that teachers have to learn more about assessments and issues such as reliability, validity, scoring, and so on. It should go without saying that the investment is well worth it.

How are formative assessments different from summative ones? In general, the same assessment can be used formatively or summatively. It's what you do with the information gained from the assessment that determines whether it's formative or summative. Consider a multiple-choice exam. Most people think of it as summative, but multiple-choice exams can be used to determine what students know and what they still need to be taught. As we discussed, when student performance results are used in a feed-forward way, the assessment is formative. When student performance results are used for a grade or for accountability, the assessment is summative.

How does formative assessment support learning? Formative assessments help teachers decide what to teach next. They also provide students with information about what they understand and still need to learn. Assessments distinguish between teaching and learning. Just because something was taught or "covered" (the term currently used) does not mean it was learned. Formative assessments, and the formative assessment system that includes feed-up, feedback, and feed-forward, should focus on student learning. It's no longer sufficient for teachers to plan and deliver lessons, hoping that students will learn. Hope is not a plan. The formative assessment system is a plan—a plan to ensure that students learn.

How do I budget time for formative assessments? It's true: There never seems to be enough time to do all of the things we want to do with and for our students. However, the formative assessment system should help teachers manage time. The whole idea of a formative assessment system is to avoid wasting time for students who already "get it" and concentrate that time on either reteaching students who still need help or advancing students' depth of understanding.

The key to implementing a formative assessment system is to keep students working, collaboratively and productively, while the teacher meets with small groups for additional instruction. The key to getting students to work together in the absence of the teacher is to teach them how to do so at the beginning of the year. Students must be taught the expectations for each productive group work task before they're asked to complete tasks together. When this has been accomplished, teachers can focus on small groups for either advanced work or review work.

We think one reason why teachers don't implement a formative assessment system is because they don't use group work; alternatively, they haven't taught students to work productively in groups. In classrooms without productive group work, the formative assessment system breaks down because the teacher has to reteach the whole class, including students who don't need it, or assign significant amounts of independent work to "keep them busy," which means that students are wasting time doing things they already know how to do.

The next question is so big that we've devoted an entire section of this chapter to it. The most common question we're asked concerns the "how" of implementing a formative assessment system. What does it take to get this implemented? What is the leader's role in providing teachers with the support they need to implement a formative assessment system? How do coaches and teacher leaders support implementation efforts?

Leadership for a Formative Assessment System

Administrators, peer coaches, and teacher leaders must complete a number of tasks, ranging from lunchtime supervision to budgets to discipline of students, all of which are necessary to keep a school operating. Unfortunately, for many of these educational leaders, pressing responsibilities related to school operations take precedence over and interfere with their ability to serve as instructional leaders. As a result, they are often prevented from spending time observing classroom instruction and talking with teachers about their professional practice.

Getting leaders into classrooms is important if school improvement efforts are to flourish; however, spending time in classrooms and providing feedback are not sufficient to create lasting change. Lasting change requires an agreement on what constitutes "high quality" so the leader and the teacher can have a productive conversation about the observation. We'll come back to this point again later, but our experiences with school improvement efforts suggest that reaching agreements on quality is crucial if professional development efforts and administrative or peer feedback are going to be effective.

As an example, think back to a conversation you've had with a teacher following a classroom observation. Say, for example, that you just returned from a conference that validated and extended your understanding of the importance of building students' background knowledge. As part of the observation, you notice several opportunities that the teacher missed to activate and build on background knowledge. The conversation you have with the teacher might go something like this:

> **Leader:** How do you think the lesson went?
>
> **Teacher:** Great, I thought that my students were all engaged.
>
> **Leader:** Yes, true, they all seemed interested in the topic. Did you think about what they might already know about the topic? Or what they might not know about the topic?
>
> **Teacher:** No, not really. I think that they learned a lot from the experience. Did you hear them talking with one another?
>
> **Leader:** Yes, they were talking and asking good questions. But what did they already know?
>
> **Teacher:** I'm not sure. But I will bet that they do well on the assessment.
>
> **Leader:** Did you think about making connections between their background knowledge and the topic at hand? Could it be that some of the students already knew this before the lesson?
>
> **Teacher:** Sure, but that's what happens in every lesson. Some students know it already, some get it, and others need more teaching.
>
> **Leader:** I think it would be useful to tap into students' background knowledge and then build on that with students.
>
> **Teacher:** Yeah, maybe. I really liked the summaries they wrote at the end. You didn't get to see that part, but I can show you what they wrote. See . . .

This conversation isn't really getting anywhere because both people have a different understanding of quality, at least in terms of the topic of background knowledge. As a result, the teacher is immune to the feedback being provided and is not likely to change as a result of the experience.

In other cases, the leader might not have a deep understanding of quality and provides feedback that is counter to what the evidence says about good teaching. That's why we think that quality is job one. Reaching agreements on what constitutes high-quality work provides a baseline from which to hold a meaningful conversation and address changes.

In our work, we focus on the four components of the gradual release of responsibility instructional framework, and we have worked to reach agreements on quality for each of them. Together, they provide an instructional framework that teachers can use to plan lessons. They also provide teachers and leaders with topics for conversation following observations.

The Quality Conversation

When teachers share a definition of quality with others at their school or district, they can have amazing conversations. When the two people having the conversation both know what they're looking for, they can compare that with what really happened in the classroom and what they'd like to do next. Here's an important point: The leader cannot simply inform teachers about specific quality indicators. That top-down style simply does not work to create lasting change. As a leader we know often says, "We're looking for commitment, not just compliance." When leaders tell teachers what quality looks like, teachers become compliant. When teachers and leaders negotiate the definition of quality together and reach new levels of understanding, teachers commit.

For example, a science teacher colleague, her peer coach, and her administrator developed an agreement on key quality indicators. Because of this, their conversation after a classroom observation is much more productive and likely to result in changes, in terms of teaching, for students, the coach, and the administrator as they work with other teachers. Unlike the conversation between the teacher and her principal in which there was not a shared definition of quality, this conversation results in reflection and growth.

> **Teacher:** I think that the students understood the purpose. Did you understand it?
>
> **Coach:** Yes, even though I wasn't a science teacher, I understood what you were expecting me to learn from the lesson. I appreciated the fact that you defined key terms as you established the purpose. But let's talk about what happened before the purpose, okay?
>
> **Teacher:** Sure. I really wanted to activate background knowledge and get students talking right away. I felt like the independent task worked and that their partner conversations helped them clarify some information.

Coach: I agree that it was useful to the students. How was it, if at all, useful to you?

Teacher: I'm not sure what you mean.

Coach: Did you use any of the information from the independent task and productive group work later in the lesson?

Teacher: I kept it in mind, but I think I know where you're going. I've told you that I would like to improve my differentiated instruction, and I think my modeling might have been more focused on what I heard students saying.

Coach: That's something to think about. Do you think students learned something important today?

Teacher: Yes, I really do. Their collaborative posters showed me which parts of the purpose they got and which I need to keep focused on.

Coach: And I have to say that your ability to guide learning through prompts and cues is impressive. It seems effortless as you help students reach new levels of understanding. I know it's not, but you make it seem so.

Teacher: Thanks. I think that I'd like to try modeling in that lesson a bit differently. Can you come to my last period class and see the difference?

Coach: Sure! I'd love to be there.

In this conversation, it is clear that both the coach and teacher share the same definition of quality, and they use that understanding to guide their conversation. In doing so, they both reach a better understanding of the teaching and learning experience. As a result, they leave the experience changed. Neither of them feels the need to defend his or her position or perspective. Instead, they have a conversation about a teaching event that is grounded in their shared understanding of an instructional framework and a formative assessment system. That's why leaders, both formal and informal, need to first engage teachers in discussions about quality. As we will see in the next section, these discussions can ensure that change actually occurs.

Going to Scale

Agreements on quality can be made at the school level or even at the district level. When these agreements are made, observations and feedback are useful in guiding conversations. This is a powerful first step in improving student achievement. In addition to the conversations these agreements foster, they can be used as a sort of needs assessment for additional professional development. For example, the staff at a local high school agreed on specific quality indicators for each component of the gradual release of responsibility framework (see Figure 6.1). This agreement provided guidance for the work of professional learning communities and resulted in specific topics scheduled for additional professional development.

When teachers at this school focused on implementing the quality indicators, they were interested in hearing what their peers and leaders thought. This common language facilitated conversations between and among teachers and provided a reason for them to plan together and observe one another. They were no longer impervious to feedback but, rather, welcomed it as an opportunity to make additional changes to their instructional repertoires. Over time, additional quality indicators were added as teachers and leaders noticed additional factors they thought should be implemented schoolwide. It should be no surprise that the achievement at this school soared, and it's now one of the highest-achieving schools in the area. Improvement came when teachers and leaders agreed on quality and started having meaningful conversations about teaching and learning. As Aristotle noted, "Quality is not an act, it is a habit." This is what agreements on quality create: habits that teachers use to ensure student understanding.

Looking Back, Looking Forward

In this chapter, we provided an overview of an instructional framework that gives teachers a structure for addressing the needs identified on formative assessments. We included information about purpose, modeling, guided instruction, productive group work, and independent tasks. Together, these constitute the gradual release of responsibility framework, which can be used to guide feed-forward efforts. We also focused on the ways in which teachers can use formative assessments to make instructional decisions, ranging from guided instruction to additional modeling or productive group work.

Figure 6.1	**Sample Quality Indicators for Each Component of the Gradual Release of Responsibility Framework**
Focus Lesson	• Purpose is explicitly presented through content and language goals, which are based on content standards, the language demands of the task, and students' needs, as identified via formative assessments. • The modeling includes naming the task or strategy, explaining when it is used, and using analogies to link to new learning. The teacher then demonstrates the task or strategy, alerts learners about errors to avoid, and shows them how it is applied to check for accuracy. The modeling consistently contains "I" statements.
Guided Instruction	• The teacher uses questions, prompts, and cues to guide students to greater understanding and does not provide students with direct explanations unless the prompts and cues fail to result in understanding. • When done with small groups, guided instruction is based on an assessed instructional need and not an artificial performance level.
Productive Group Work	• The task is a novel application of a grade-level-appropriate concept and is designed so that the outcome is not guaranteed (i.e., a chance for productive failure exists). • Small groups of 2–5 students are purposefully constructed to maximize individual strengths without magnifying areas of need (heterogeneous grouping).
Independent Learning Tasks	• The task is a novel application that relates to the purpose of the lesson and provides students with an opportunity to apply what they have learned. • Students practice with their peers before being asked to complete tasks independently. • Student responses to independent tasks are used to make future instructional decisions, such as whole-class reteaching and additional guided instruction.

We answered some commonly asked questions about a formative assessment system and provided guidance for leaders about implementing such a system. Our discussion focused on the importance of a mutually understood definition of quality and how this agreement will facilitate conversations that create change.

Looking forward, we hope to see formative assessment systems drive reform and school improvement. The work that students do at school can, and should, be used to guide future instructional actions. We also look forward to teachers balancing between feedback and feed-forward, not relying solely on feedback to improve student understanding. Finally, we look forward to improvements on our model as we learn from our students and colleagues, and perhaps from you, as we continue the quest to ensure that all students learn in environments that are responsive to their individual needs.

We've come to the end of this book but not the end of the work on a formative assessment system. It's ongoing and becomes a way of life for teachers who want to ensure that they use student performance information to ensure that all students learn. Far be it from us to imply that creating and implementing a formative assessment system is easy. It's not. It's very hard work, rife with setbacks and frustrations.

This reality reminds us of a meeting we attended several years ago in which we were told that there would be a new computer program used for intervention. The promise from the salesperson was that teachers could keep teaching new material while the software did all the reteaching. It was appealing, and some of our colleagues thought it would work; computers are a great resource to have in the classroom. The system our school bought, however, did not result in breakthrough results. Machines cannot provide all of the reteaching students need. Teachers had to determine what students understood and what they still needed to learn. When we used the computer system as an adjunct to our formative assessment system, the results were better.

The same thing happened during Doug's quest to run a marathon. Several months into his training, Doug hurt his knee and had to make midcourse corrections. He temporarily hired a coach to analyze his run and provide additional instruction. It turned out that Doug was overpronating (i.e., turning his foot inward when it landed). With some additional instruction, and new running shoes, Doug was back on track to meet his goal.

"The Computer Year," as we now call it, was a minor setback in our journey toward implementing a formative assessment system at our school. We've had a lot of successes and know that we are better teachers because of them. Sure, we made mistakes, but we had to get started—and that's what we hope you'll do. Try out the ideas contained in this book. Think about a lesson's purpose and how it's communicated to students. Consider the various ways to check for understanding, and implement some of them. Change your focus on feedback and include some feed-forward instruction. It won't be perfect, or necessarily easy, at first, but it will begin to change your teaching repertoire and meet your students' needs more quickly and more often.

References

Airasian, P. W. (1997). *Classroom assessment* (3rd ed.). New York: McGraw-Hill.

Alfassi, M. (2004). Reading to learn: The effects of combined strategies instruction on high school students. *Journal of Educational Research, 97*(4), 171–184.

Allen, M. (2010). Learner error, affectual simulation, and conceptual change. *Journal of Research in Science Teaching, 47*(2), 151–173.

Anderson, J. R. (1983). *The architecture of cognition.* Cambridge, MA: Harvard University Press.

Anderson, L. W., & Krathwohl, D. R. (Eds.) (2001). *A taxonomy for learning, teaching, and assessing: A revision of Bloom's taxonomy of educational objectives.* Boston: Allyn & Bacon.

Arzarello, F., Paola, F., Robutti, O., & Sabena, C. (2009). Gestures as semiotic resources in the mathematics classroom. *Educational Studies in Mathematics, 70*(2), 97–109.

Asher, J. (2007). *Thirteen reasons why.* New York: Razorbill.

Au, K. H. (2010). Help students take charge of their literacy learning. *Reading Today, 27*(4), 18.

Au, K. H., Carroll, J. H., & Scheu, J. R. (1995). *Balanced literacy instruction: A teacher's resource book.* Norwood, MA: Christopher-Gordon.

Austen, J. (1996). *Pride and prejudice.* H. Bloom (Ed.). Broomall, PA: Chelsea House Publishers.

Babbitt, N. (1975). *Tuck everlasting.* New York: Farrar, Straus, Giroux.

Bandura, A. (1965). Influence of models' reinforcement contingencies on the acquisition of imitative responses. *Journal of Personality and Social Psychology, 1,* 589–595.

Bangert-Downs, R. L., Kulik, C. C., Kulik, J. A., & Morgan, M. (1991). The instructional effects of feedback in test-like events. *Review of Educational Research, 61*(2), 213–238.

Bartoletti, S. C. (2005). *Hitler youth: Growing up in Hitler's shadow.* New York: Scholastic.

Bereiter, D., & Engelmann, S. (1966). *Teaching disadvantaged children in the preschool.* Boston: Allyn & Bacon.

Bloom, B. B. (1956). *Taxonomy of educational objectives, handbook 1: Cognitive domain.* New York: Addison Wesley Publishing Company.

Bong, M. (2008). Effects of parent–child relationships and classroom goal structures on motivation, help-seeking avoidance, and cheating. *Journal of Experimental Education, 76,* 191–217.

Boyne, J. (2006). *The boy in the striped pajamas.* New York: David Fickling Books.

Bransford, J. D., Brown, A. L., & Cocking, R. C. (Eds.). (2000). *How people learn: Brain, mind, experience, and school.* Washington, DC: National Academy Press.

Brookhart, S. M. (2008). *How to give effective feedback to your students.* Alexandria, VA: ASCD.

Burnett, P. C. (2002). Teacher praise and feedback and students' perceptions of the classroom environment. *Educational Psychology, 22*(1), 1–16.

California Department of Education. (n.d.). *Common benchmark assessments.* Retrieved from http://pubs.cde.ca.gov/TCSII/ch2/comnbnchmrkassess.aspx

Cazden, C. B. (1988). *Classroom discourse: The language of teaching and learning.* Portsmouth, NH: Heinemann.

Chi, M. T. H., Siler, S. A., & Jeong, H. (2004). Can tutors monitor students' understanding accurately? *Cognition and Instruction, 22*(3), 363–387.

Clay, M. (2010). *Running records for classroom teachers.* Portsmouth, NH: Heinemann.

Covey, S. R. (2004). *The 7 habits of highly effective people: Powerful lessons in personal change* (Rev. ed.). New York: Free Press.

Crawford, M. B. (2009). *Shop class as soulcraft.* New York: Penguin.

Duckworth, A. L., Petersen, C., Matthews, M. D., & Kelly, D. R. (2007). Grit: Persistence and passion for long-term goals. *Journal of Personality and Social Psychology, 92,* 1087–1101.

Duffy, G. G. (2003). *Explaining reading: A resource for teaching concepts, skills, and strategies.* New York: Guilford.

Dufrene, B. A., Noell, G. H., & Gilbertson, D. N. (2005). Monitoring implementation of reciprocal peer tutoring: Identifying and intervening with students who do not maintain accurate implementation. *School Psychology Review, 34*(1), 74–86.

Duke, N. K., & Pearson, P. D. (2004). Effective practices for developing reading comprehension. In A. E. Farstup & S. J. Samuels (Eds.), *What research has to say about reading instruction* (pp. 205–242). Newark, DE: International Reading Association.

Dutro, S., & Moran, C. (2003). Rethinking English language instruction: An architectural approach. In G. Garcia (Ed.), *English learners: Reaching the highest level of English literacy* (pp. 227–258). Newark, DE: International Reading Association.

Dweck, C. S. (2007). The perils and promises of praise. *Educational Leadership, 65*(2), 34–39.

Elbow, P. (1994). *Writing for learning—not just for demonstrating learning.* University of Massachusetts, Amherst. Available: http://www.ntlf.com/html/lib/bib/writing.htm

Ellis, R. (2009). A typology of written corrective feedback types. *ELT Journal, 63*(2), 97–107.

Emmer, E. T., & Evertson, C. M. (2008). *Classroom management for middle and high school teachers* (8th ed.). Boston: Allyn & Bacon.

Fearn, L., & Farnan, N. (2001). *Interactions: Teaching writing and language arts.* Boston: Allyn & Bacon.

Ferris, D. (2006). Does error feedback help student writers? New evidence on the short- and long-term effects of written error correction. In K. Hyland & F. Hyland (Eds.), *Feedback in second language writing: Contexts and issues* (pp. 81–104). Cambridge: Cambridge University Press.

Ferris, D. R. (1997). The influence of teacher commentary on student revision. *TESOL Quarterly, 31*(2), 315–333.

Field, J. (2008). Bricks or mortar: Which parts of the input does a second language learner rely on? *TESOL Quarterly, 42*(3), 411–432.

Fisher, D., & Frey, N. (2007a). *Checking for understanding: Formative assessment techniques for your classroom.* Alexandria, VA: ASCD.

Fisher, D., & Frey, N. (2007b). Implementing a schoolwide literacy framework: Improving achievement in an urban elementary school. *The Reading Teacher, 61,* 32–45.

Fisher, D., & Frey, N. (2007c). *Scaffolding writing: A gradual release approach to writing instruction.* New York: Scholastic.

Fisher, D., & Frey, N. (2008a). *Better learning through structured teaching: A framework for the gradual release of responsibility.* Alexandria, VA: ASCD.

Fisher, D., & Frey, N. (2008b). *Improving adolescent literacy: Content area reading strategies at work* (2nd ed.). Upper Saddle River, NJ: Merrill Prentice Hall.

Fisher, D., & Frey, N. (2010). *Guided instruction: How to develop confident and successful learners.* Alexandria, VA: ASCD.

Fisher, D., Frey, N., & Grant, M. (2009). A diploma that matters: Schoolwide efforts to improve high school teaching and learning. In S. R. Parris, D. Fisher, & K. Headley (Eds.), *Adolescent literacy, field-tested: Effective solutions for every classroom* (pp. 191–203). Newark, DE: International Reading Association.

Fisher, D., Frey, N., & Rothenberg, C. (2008). *Content area conversations: How to plan discussion-based lessons for diverse language learners.* Alexandria, VA: ASCD.

Fountas, I. C., & Pinnell, G. S. (2001). *Guiding readers and writers: Teaching comprehension, genre, and content literacy.* Portsmouth, NH: Heinemann.

Frey, N. (2010). *The effective teacher's guide. 50 ways to engage students and promote interactive learning* (2nd ed.). New York: Guilford.

Frey, N., & Fisher, D. (2006). *Language arts workshop: Purposeful reading and writing instruction.* Upper Saddle River, NJ: Merrill Prentice Hall.

Frey, N., Fisher, D., & Everlove, S. (2009). *Productive group work: How to engage students, build teamwork, and promote understanding.* Alexandria, VA: ASCD.

Frey, N., Fisher, D., & Hernandez, T. (2003). What's the gist? Summary writing for struggling adolescent writers. *Voices from the Middle, 11*(2), 43–49.

Frey, N., Fisher, D., & Moore, K. (2009). Literacy letters: Comparative literature and formative assessment. *The ALAN Review, 36*(2), 27–33.

Fuchs, D., Fuchs, L. S., & Burish, P. (2000). Peer-assisted learning strategies: An evidence-based practice to promote reading achievement. *Learning Disabilities Research and Practice, 15*(2), 85–91.

Gambrell, L., Koskinen, P. S., & Kapinus, B. A. (1991). Retellling and the reading comprehension of proficient and less-proficient readers. *Journal of Educational Research, 84,* 356–362.

Gawande, A. (2009). *The checklist manifesto: How to get things right.* New York: Metropolitan.

Girgin, U. (2006). Evaluation of Turkish hearing-impaired students' reading comprehension with the miscue analysis inventory. *International Journal of Special Education, 21*(3), 68–84.

Good, T. L., & Brophy, J. E. (2007). *Looking in classrooms* (10th ed.). Boston: Allyn & Bacon.

Goodman, K. S. (1967). A psycholinguistic guessing game. *Journal of the Reading Specialist, 6,* 126–135.

Goodman, Y. M., & Burke, C. L. (1972). *Reading miscue inventory.* Katonah, NY: Richard C. Owen.

Harter, S. (1998). The development of self-representations. In W. Damon (Series Ed.) & N. Eisenberg (Vol. Ed.), *Handbook of child psychology: Vol. 3. Social, emotional, and personality development* (5th ed., pp. 553–617). New York: Wiley.

Hattie, J. (2009). *Visible learning: A synthesis of over 800 meta-analyses relating to achievement.* New York: Routledge.

Hattie, J., & Marsh, H. W. (1995). Future research in self-concept. In B. Bracken (Ed.), *Handbook on self-concept* (pp. 421–463). Hillsdale, NJ: Lawrence Erlbaum.

Hattie, J., & Timperley, H. (2007). The power of feedback. *Review of Educational Research, 77,* 81–112.

Hogan, K., & Pressley, M. (1997). Scaffolding scientific competencies within classroom communities of inquiry. In K. Hogan & M. Pressley (Eds.), *Scaffolding student learning: Instructional approaches and issues* (pp. 74–107). Cambridge, MA: Brookline.

Jacobson, J., Thrope, L., Fisher, D., Lapp, D., Frey, N., & Flood, J. (2001). Cross-age tutoring: A literacy improvement approach for struggling adolescent readers. *Journal of Adolescent and Adult Literacy, 44,* 528–536.

Johnson, D. W., & Johnson, R. T. (1999). *Learning together and alone: Cooperative, competitive, and individualistic learning* (5th ed.). Needham Heights, MA: Allyn & Bacon.

Justice, L. M. (2006). *Communicate sciences and disorders: An introduction.* Upper Saddle River, NJ: Merrill Prentice Hall.

Kendeou, P., & van den Broek, P. (2005). The effects of readers' misconceptions on comprehension of scientific text. *Journal of Educational Psychology, 97*(2), 235–245.

Kidd, S. M. (2002). *The secret life of bees.* New York: Viking.

Klein, W. M. (2001). Post hoc construction of self-performance and other performance in self-serving social comparison. *Society for Personality and Social Psychology, 27*(6), 744–754.

Kluger, A. N., & DeNisi, A. (1998). Feedback interventions: Towards the understanding of a double-edged sword. *Current Directions in Psychological Science, 7*, 67–72.

Kramarski, B., & Zoldan, S. (2008). Using errors as springboards for enhancing mathematical reasoning with three metacognitive approaches. *The Journal of Educational Research, 102*(2), 137–151.

Krull, E., Oras, K., & Sisack, S. (2007). Differences in teachers' comments on classroom events as indicators of their professional development. *Teaching and Teacher Education, 23*, 1038–1050.

Langer, J. A. (2001). Beating the odds: Teaching middle and high school students to read and write well. *American Educational Research Journal, 38*, 837–880.

Larkin, M. (2002). *Using scaffolded instruction to optimize learning.* Arlington, VA: ERIC Clearinghouse on Disabilities and Gifted Education. Retrieved from http://www.ericdigests.org/2003-5/optimize.htm

Lee, I. (2009). Ten mismatches between teachers' beliefs and written feedback practice. *ELT Journal, 63*(1), 13–22.

Lyman, F. T. (1981). The responsive classroom discussion: The inclusion of all students. In A. Anderson (Ed.), *Mainstreaming digest* (pp. 109–113). College Park: University of Maryland Press.

Mansell, J., Evans, M., & Hamilton-Hulak, L. (2005). Developmental changes in parents' use of miscue feedback during shared book reading. *Reading Research Quarterly, 40*(3), 294–317.

Marzano, R., Pickering, D., & Pollock, J. (2001). *Classroom instruction that works: Research-based strategies for increasing student achievement.* Alexandria, VA: ASCD.

Mastropieri, M. A., Scruggs, T., Mohler, L., Beranek, M., Spencer, V., Boon, R. T., & Talbot, E. (2001). Can middle school students with serious reading difficulties help each other and learn anything? *Learning Disabilities Research and Practice, 16*, 18–27.

McTighe, J., & O'Connor, K. (2005). Seven practices for effective learning. *Educational Leadership, 63*(3), 10–17.

Moore, R., & Brantingham, K. (2003). Nathan: A case study in reader response and retrospective miscue analysis. *The Reading Teacher, 56*(5), 466–474.

Myers, W. D. (2004). *Monster.* New York: HarperTempest.

Nagy, W. E., Anderson, R. C., & Herman, P. A. (1987). Learning word meanings from context during normal reading. *American Educational Research Journal, 24*, 237–270.

Nelson-Le Gall, S. (1985). Help-seeking behavior in learning. In E. W. Gordon (Ed.), *Review of research in education* (Vol. 12, pp. 55–90). Washington, DC: American Educational Research Association.

Palincsar, A. S., & Brown, A. L. (1984). Reciprocal teaching of comprehension-fostering and comprehension-monitoring activities. *Cognition and Instruction, 1*(1), 117–175.

Paris, S. G., & Winograd, P. (1990). Promoting metacognition and motivation of exceptional children. *Remedial and Special Education, 11*(6), 7–15.

Pausch, R. (2008). *The last lecture.* New York: Hyperion.

Pearson, P. D., & Gallagher, G. (1983). The gradual release of responsibility model of instruction. *Contemporary Educational Psychology, 8,* 112–123.

Piaget, J. (1952). *The origins of intelligence in children.* New York: W. W. Norton & Co.

Pianta, R. C., LaParo, K. M., & Hamre, B. K. (2008). *Classroom assessment scoring system (K–3).* Baltimore, MD: Paul H. Brookes.

Ping, R. M., & Goldin-Meadow, S. (2008). Hands in the air: Using ungrounded iconic gestures to teach children conservation of quantity. *Developmental Psychology, 44*(5), 1277–1287.

Raphael, T. E. (1986). Teaching question–answer relationships, revisited. *The Reading Teacher, 39,* 198–205.

Rauschenbach, J. (1994). Checking for student understanding: Four techniques. *Physical Education, Recreation, and Dance, 65*(4), 60–63.

Rice, M. L., Smolik, F., Perpich, D., Thompson, T., Rytting, N., & Blossom, M. (2010). Mean length utterance levels in 6-month intervals for children 3 to 9 years with and without language impairments. *Journal of Speech, Language, and Hearing Research, 53*(2), 333–349.

Rohrer, D., & Pashler, H. (2010). Recent research on human learning challenges conventional instructional strategies. *Educational Researcher, 39*(5), 406–412.

Ross, P., & Gibson, S. A. (2010). Exploring a conceptual framework for expert noticing in literacy instruction. *Literacy Research and Instruction, 49,* 175–193.

Ryan, R. M., & Deci, E. L. (2000). Self-determination theory and the facilitation of intrinsic motivation, social development, and well-being. *American Psychologist, 55,* 68–78.

Santa, C., & Havens, L. (1995). *Creating independence through student-owned strategies: Project CRISS.* Dubuque, IA: Kendall-Hunt.

Scheeler, M. C., Macluckie, M., & Albright, K. (2010). Effects of immediate feedback on the oral presentation skills of adolescents with learning disabilities. *Remedial and Special Education, 31*(2), 77–86.

Shaw, D. (2005). *Retelling strategies to improve comprehension: Effective hands-on strategies for fiction and nonfiction that help students remember and understand what they read.* New York: Scholastic.

Siedentop, D. (1991). *Developing teaching skills in physical education* (3rd ed.). Mountainview, CA: Mayfield.

Simmons, J. (2003). Responders are taught, not born. *Journal of Adolescent and Adult Literacy, 46*(8), 684–693.

Stronge, J. H. (2007). *Qualities of effective teachers* (2nd ed.). Alexandria, VA: ASCD.

Taylor, W. L. (1953). Cloze procedure: A new tool for measuring readability. *Journalism Quarterly, 30,* 415–433.

Tienken, C. H., Goldberg, S., & DiRocco, D. (2009). Questioning the questions. *Kappa Delta Pi Record, 46*(1), 39–43.

Tomlinson, C. A. (2001). *How to differentiate instruction in mixed-ability classrooms* (2nd ed.). Alexandria, VA: ASCD.

Treglia, M. O. (2008). Feedback on feedback: Exploring student responses to teachers' written commentary. *Journal of Basic Writing, 27*(1), 105–137.

Vygotsky, L. S. (1962). *Thought and language*. Cambridge, MA: MIT Press.

Vygotsky, L. S. (1978). *Mind in society*. Cambridge, MA: Harvard University Press.

White, E. B. (1952). *Charlotte's web*. New York: Harper & Row.

Wiggins, G. (1998). *Educative assessment: Designing assessments to inform and improve student performance*. San Francisco: Jossey-Bass.

Wood, D., Bruner, J. S., & Ross, G. (1976). The role of tutoring and problem solving. *Journal of Child Psychology and Psychiatry, 17*, 89–100.

Wurr, A., Theurer, J., & Kim, K. (2008). Retrospective miscue analysis with proficient adult ESL readers. *Journal of Adolescent and Adult Literacy, 52*(4), 324–333.

Zimmerman, B. J. (1990). Self-regulated learning and academic achievement: An overview. *Educational Psychologist, 25*, 3–17.

Zimmerman, B. J. (2000). Attaining self-regulation: A social cognitive perspective. In M. Boekaerts & P. R. Pintrich (Eds.), *Handbook of self-regulation: Research, theory, and applications* (pp. 13–39). San Diego: Academic Press.

Zwiers, J. (2008). *Building academic language: Essential practices for content classrooms*. San Francisco: Jossey-Bass.

Index

The letter *f* following a page number denotes a figure.

About the Authors

Nancy Frey, PhD, is a professor of literacy in the School of Teacher Education at San Diego State University and a teacher leader at Health Sciences High and Middle College. Before joining the university faculty, Nancy was a special education teacher in the Broward County (Florida) Public Schools, where she taught students at the elementary and middle school levels. She later worked for the Florida Department of Education on a statewide project for supporting students with disabilities in a general education curriculum. Nancy is a recipient of the Christa McAuliffe Award for Excellence in Teacher Education from the American Association of State Colleges and Universities and the Early Career Award from the National Reading Conference. Her research interests include reading and literacy, assessment, intervention, and curriculum design. She has published many articles and books on literacy and instruction, including *Productive Group Work and Better Learning Through Structured Teaching*. She can be reached at nfrey@mail.sdsu.edu.

Douglas Fisher, PhD, is a professor of language and literacy education in the Department of Teacher Education at San Diego State University and a teacher leader at Health Sciences High and Middle College. He is a member of the California Reading Hall of Fame and is the recipient of a Celebrate Literacy Award from the International Reading Association, the Farmer Award for Excellence in Writing from the National Council of Teachers of English, and a Christa McAuliffe Award for Excellence in Teacher Education from the American Association of State Colleges and Universities. He has published numerous articles on improving student achievement, and his books include *Enhancing RTI: How to Ensure Success with Effective Classroom Instruction and Intervention, Checking for Understanding,* and *Content-Area Conversations.* He can be reached at dfisher@mail.sdsu.edu.

Related ASCD Resources: Formative Assessment

At the time of publication, the following ASCD resources were available (ASCD stock numbers appear in parentheses). For up-to-date information about ASCD resources, go to www.ascd.org. You can search the complete archives of *Educational Leadership* at http://www.ascd.org/el.

ASCD Edge Group
Exchange ideas and connect with other educators interested in formative assessment on the social networking site ASCD Edge™ at http://ascdedge.ascd.org/

Multimedia
Formative Assessment Strategies for Every Classroom (2nd Ed.): An ASCD Action Tool by Susan M. Brookhart (#111005)

Online Professional Development
Formative Assessment: The Basics (#PD09OC69). Visit the ASCD website (www.ascd.org).

Print Products
Advancing Formative Assessment in Every Classroom: A Guide for Instructional Leaders by Connie M. Moss and Susan M. Brookhart (#109031)

Checking for Understanding: Formative Assessment Techniques for Your Classroom by Douglas Fisher and Nancy Frey (#107023)

Exploring Formative Assessment (The Professional Learning Community Series) by Susan M. Brookhart (#109038)

Transformative Assessment by W. James Popham (#108018)

What Teachers Really Need to Know About Formative Assessment by Laura Greenstein (#110017)

Video
Formative Assessment in Content Areas (series of three 25-minute DVDs, each with a professional development program) (#609034)

Formative Assessment in Content Areas—Elementary School (one 25-minute DVD with a professional development program) (#609098)

Formative Assessment in Content Areas—Middle School (one 25-minute DVD with a professional development program) (#609099)

Formative Assessment in Content Areas—High School (one 25-minute DVD with a professional development program) (#609100)

The Power of Formative Assessment to Advance Learning (series of three 25- to 30-minute DVDs, with a comprehensive user guide) (#608066)

THE WHOLE CHILD The Whole Child Initiative helps schools and communities create learning environments that allow students to be healthy, safe, engaged, supported, and challenged. To learn more about other books and resources that relate to the whole child, visit www.wholechildeducation.org.

For more information: send e-mail to member@ascd.org; call 1-800-933-2723 or 703-578-9600, press 2; send a fax to 703-575-5400; or write to Information Services, ASCD, 1703 N. Beauregard St., Alexandria, VA 22311-1714 USA.